UNDERSTANDING BUYING AND SELLING A HOUSE
Revised Edition

This book explains:

* ★ The hows, wheres and whys of home buying and selling
* ★ How to make the most money when selling your house
* ★ How to get the best deal when buying your house
* ★ The ins and outs of mortgages, escrow and closing
* ★ Why real estate can be such a profitable investment

THE NO NONSENSE LIBRARY

NO NONSENSE FINANCIAL GUIDES

How to Finance Your Child's College Education
How to Use Credit and Credit Cards, Revised Edition
Understanding Tax-Exempt Bonds, Revised Edition
Understanding Money Market Funds, Revised Edition
Understanding Mutual Funds, Revised Edition
Understanding IRA's, Revised Edition
Understanding Treasury Bills and Other U.S. Government Securities, Revised Edition
Understanding Common Stocks, Revised Edition
Understanding the Stock Market, Revised Edition
Understanding Stock Options and Futures Markets, Revised Edition
How to Choose a Discount Stockbroker, Revised Edition
How to Make Personal Financial Planning Work for You, Revised Edition
How to Plan and Invest for Your Retirement, Revised Edition
The New Tax Law and What It Means to You

NO NONSENSE REAL ESTATE GUIDES

Understanding Condominiums and Co-ops, Revised Edition
Understanding Buying and Selling a House, Revised Edition
Understanding Mortgages and Home Equity Loans, Revised Edition
Refinancing Your Mortgage, Revised Edition

NO NONSENSE LEGAL GUIDES

Understanding Estate Planning and Wills, Revised Edition
How to Choose a Lawyer

NO NONSENSE CAREER GUIDES

How to Use Your Time Wisely
Managing People

NO NONSENSE SUCCESS GUIDES

NO NONSENSE HEALTH GUIDES

NO NONSENSE COOKING GUIDES

NO NONSENSE WINE GUIDES

NO NONSENSE PARENTING GUIDES

NO NONSENSE REAL ESTATE GUIDE™

UNDERSTANDING BUYING AND SELLING A HOUSE

Revised Edition

Phyllis C. Kaufman
& Arnold Corrigan

LONGMEADOW PRESS

To
Beth Greenspun
A Friend For
All Seasons

The authors want to thank real estate developer and lecturer Jack W. Blumenfeld, without whose advice, help and wisdom this book would not have been possible.

This publication is designed to provide accurate and authoritative information with regard to the subject matter covered. It is sold with the understanding that neither the publisher nor the authors are engaged in rendering legal, accounting, or other professional service regarding the subject matter covered. If legal advice or other expert assistance is desired, the services of a competent professional person should be sought.

Understanding Buying and Selling a House, Revised Edition

CONTENTS

PART I
FOR BUYERS
AND SELLERS

1

HOUSE FOR SALE

Psychologists tell us that, along with marriage, divorce, and death of a loved one, buying or selling a house is one of the most traumatic experiences of a lifetime. However, it doesn't necessarily have to be that way. You can avoid trauma simply by understanding what to do and how to approach each phase of the buying or selling process.

Understanding Buying and Selling a House will take you through the basics of home purchase and sale. After the introductory chapters, the book is divided into two sections, one primarily for buyers and one for sellers. But while one section may be more relevant to you at the moment than the other, we suggest that you read both. You will be a better buyer if you understand what the seller is thinking and doing—and vice versa.

Our first piece of advice is *be prepared!* Buying or selling a house is a major transaction. At each step of the way you must spend time thinking and organizing. We will give you all the help we can. But you must do your homework and take the time to do it right.

2

THE PLAYERS IN THE REAL ESTATE GAME

The players in the real estate game are, obviously, the buyer and the seller. Let's take a moment to look at each one's goals.

The Buyer

The buyer wants to buy the very best house, in the most stable and prosperous neighborhood, for the least amount of money. The buyer is worried about the physical condition of the house, the price to be paid, and the effect of this huge purchase on his or her lifestyle.

The Seller

The seller wants to unload a house he or she has outgrown or for some reason no longer wants to occupy, in exchange for the most money possible. The seller wants to minimize or hide any existing flaws and maximize the good points of the property.

The Real Estate Lawyer

Each party to the purchase of a house should engage a lawyer who specializes in real estate transactions to make sure that all legal papers, including the title, agreements and closing documents, are in order. Throughout this book you will see how a good real estate lawyer can ease the path to a successful purchase or sale.

The Title Company

In most states, the title company is called upon to research the title (legal ownership) to the property. This research is needed to establish that there is no flaw in the chain of ownership, and that there is no claim that would interfere with the present owner's ability to pass good title (ownership) to the buyer. The buyer is the one to engage and pay the title company, and he or she usually also purchases title insurance through the title company—insurance against any flaw in the title that might later be discovered. In some states, the function performed by a title company is done by a specialized attorney.

The Mortgage

The mortgage is the document—actually, a *pledge*—given by the buyer to the person or company who lends him or her the money needed to purchase the property. The loan is really called a *mortgage loan.* In exchange for the loan, the buyer promises to repay the lender the principal, plus interest at a rate determined in the mortgage agreement, and *pledges* the property as security for the repayment of the loan. If the buyer fails in the repayment, the lender has the right to foreclose (take legal possession of) the property.

Governmental Agencies
FHA

The Federal Housing Authority (FHA) is a part of the U.S. Department of Housing and Urban Development (HUD). It encourages home ownership with loan insurance programs that can help you get 30-year mortgage loans with a small down payment (often only 3%). There are no specific economic requirements for FHA assistance, but the property, which may be new or existing, rural or urban, must meet the HUD Minimum Property Standards and must be priced within the FHA limitations. The price limitations vary from area to area, with the basic limit on a single-family home at about $67,500.

The FHA also has specialized programs to assist displaced persons or those who have been the victims of disasters. Your local HUD Field Office will supply you with a complete program list as well as several informative pamphlets.

All FHA mortgages are assumable. This means that if you decide to sell your house, the buyer will be able to take over your mortgage at your interest rate (which hopefully will be lower than the going rate at the time of resale).

VA

The Veterans Administration (VA) guarantees that eligible veterans will be able to get mortgages with no money down, and if the veteran defaults, the VA will pay off the mortgage loan. Like FHA loans, VA loans are assumable.

FmHA

Farmers Home Administration (FmHA) loans are available to farmers and to nonfarmers who live within alloted rural areas and who meet the low-income requirements. The FmHA is part of the U.S. Department of Agriculture.

State and Local Governments

Finally, some state and local governments have become active in the mortgage business, offering special low interest, low down payment deals to qualified low-income buyers. Others distribute mortgage money through a lottery system, with qualified buyers receiving money by the luck of the draw.

3

REAL ESTATE BROKERS

Real estate brokers, agents and realtors are important enough to both the buyer and the seller of a house to deserve a separate chapter.

Hired and paid for by the seller, it is the job of the agent or broker to bring potential buyers to see the property the seller has for sale. A real estate broker, called a realtor in some states, has passed an examination and holds a state license which allows him or her to show houses to potential buyers and to negotiate purchases, for a fee paid by the seller. The broker or realtor usually employs salespersons who are also licensed by the state.

Experience and Professionalism

The key words to remember when dealing with a real estate broker or salesperson are (1) experience and (2) reputation for professionalism. This chapter will explain how to find people to assist you in the purchase or sale of a house who meet these two criteria.

Commission

Not all real estate transactions make use of brokers. Many people sell their houses themselves, through advertising or word of mouth. These sellers save the realtor's commission. We will talk more in Chapter 19 about selling your house without a broker. For now, it is important for everyone to understand what a broker is and how a broker operates.

As we said, the seller pays the broker's commission. This commission is usually 6% of the sale price, although the percentage can vary, depending on the custom of the area. Always check the broker's commission rates before you sign any agreements with him or her. And it is a good idea to confirm the percentage with the local board of realtors and to check newspaper ads or other brokers, just to make sure that you aren't committing to paying higher than the going rate.

The agents or salespersons who are employed by the broker are usually compensated by some combination of salary, plus a portion of the commission on any sales they actually make.

Becoming a Real Estate Broker

Let us look at how someone gets into the real estate business. Each state has its own rules and regulations regarding the examinations and requirements for licensing. In most states, the first step is to become a "salesperson" or "agent" by passing an examination. The salesperson or agent is not yet qualified to act as an independent broker, but is qualified to be employed by a broker. A broker is someone who has worked a required number of years in real estate and has taken additional courses and another more difficult examination. A broker is qualified to run a real estate business, to negotiate the sale of houses and other properties, and to receive fees for his or her efforts.

A real estate broker's license, therefore, is more difficult to get, requiring professional experience, education and a state examination. A broker may also be a realtor, that is, a member of the National Association of Realtors, a trade association whose goal is to raise the professional level of the business. "Realists" are members of a trade association to promote minority rights called the National Association of Real Estate Brokers.

Your daily dealings will usually be with an agent or salesperson rather than with the broker. Make sure that you have a good rapport with your salesperson. If you have any doubts, ask the broker to change your salesperson. Don't hesitate to speak up if you are dissatisfied. Remember that the brokers want to keep your listing in their office and want you to be satisfied. They expect that you will tell your friends of their service, and your satisfaction is important to their reputation.

The reputation of the broker and his or her associates is as important to the buyer as the seller, because a competent professional is less likely to lead you to houses that are unsuitable for you or that you can't afford. Even though paid by the seller, a good broker keeps the best interest of all parties in mind.

Finding a Broker

How do you find a competent broker? First, check with friends and acquaintances. A personal reference from a satisfied client is always the best referral. Second, if you intend to buy and have selected the neighborhood in which you are interested, drive around the area and see whose signs appear most frequently. Ask people who live in the area for names.

Third, don't fail to call the local board of realtors and make sure that the broker you select is a member. In most areas, the local realty board will supply you with a list of its members.

Of course, just because a broker is a member of a local board doesn't mean that the broker necessarily meets our two criteria of experience and professionalism. But a local board is likely to police its members and keep its standards high. If you combine membership with personal recommendations, you stand a reasonable chance of finding an experienced and competent professional.

Fourth, if a multiple listing service (MLS) is available in the area, make sure that the broker you select is a member. (See Chapter 19.) This will ensure you a wide variety of houses to look at.

Conflict of Interest

As we said, the broker is paid by the seller but also represents the buyer. This dual capacity carries a potential for conflict, and is another reason to make sure that you choose an agent with a good reputation. Keep in mind that the agent will do a certain amount of negotiating and that the parties for whom he or she is acting as intermediary, the buyer and the seller, have opposite and conflicting goals. The seller wants to receive the most money, the buyer wants to pay the least money. So, no matter which party you are, remember this dual capacity and potential for conflict whenever you confide in "your" broker or agent.

Broker Services

There are several services that a broker performs. The most obvious is to bring potential buyers to a house. The second is to pay for advertising the house in as many newspapers as he or she thinks prudent. The third is to place the house on the multiple listing service (MLS), if one is available.

Buyer-Agents

The buyer doesn't have to sign any documents with the average broker. However, a new crop of brokers is emerging now, called buyer-agents. These agents are hired and paid by the buyer. They charge either a fixed fee equal to a percentage of the sale price, or an upfront fee, payable upon signing a contract, and an hourly fee to follow, or a combination of all three.

The advantage of a buyer-agent is apparent in a very tight market where not many houses are available, or when you have a very limited time in which to find the right house and move in. It is usual for buyer-agents also to negotiate for you, which does away with the traditional conflict of interest that exists because one agent is acting for both buyer and seller. In this case, each party now has his or her own personal representative.

You can get a list of buyer-agents from the local board, or you can purchase *Who's Who in Creative Real Estate* by sending $25.00 to 921 E. Main Street, Suite F, Ventura, California 93001. This book is a national directory with a list of about 1,200 buyer-agents.

Custom

Many areas of real estate transactions are governed by state or local laws. However, some things are done in a certain way according to local custom. This is true, for example, in deciding which items are paid for by which party at closing, and how much money is required as a "good faith" deposit.

A competent real estate agent will be able to tell you about local custom. However, remember that custom is just that. It is not law, and it can be altered in a given case.

PART II
BUYING A HOUSE

4

ADVANTAGES AND DISADVANTAGES OF OWNERSHIP

The decision to buy a house, rather than to continue to rent or live rent-free with parents or friends, is probably the biggest economic decision you will ever make. The responsibility of knowing that every month, for the next 20 or 30 years, you will have to pay a considerable sum of money for your housing can be awesome.

Advantages of Ownership

Yet the advantages of ownership are exciting: the pride of owning your own property, of knowing that every improvement you make is for your own benefit, and the security of knowing that, as long as you make your monthly payments on time, you can live in your house for as long as you like. In addition, the privacy and security of a house and the inability of others to intrude on your lifestyle are all arguments in favor of ownership.

And a house is an attractive financial investment. You can take federal income tax deductions for your mortgage interest (on your primary or secondary residence) and for your real estate tax payments. And your mortgage payments steadily increase your equity in a long-term investment that you can sell after you no longer want to live there.

Finally, real estate is an investment that in the vast majority of cases appreciates, that is, goes up in value, over time. So owning your own house is also a hedge against inflation.

Leveraging

Also consider that when you buy a house, you are leveraging your money. Leveraging means that, with a small (15% to 20%) down payment, you can purchase an expensive property. You have parlayed your 20% down payment into 100% ownership.

In addition, though monthly mortgage payments may be more expensive than rent, you can often use your first house to "trade up," that is, to sell the first house at a profit and to invest the profit in a second and more expensive house, and so on. This is leveraging used to best advantage.

Disadvantages of Ownership

Of course, there are also disadvantages to buying. You are tying up your money in a nonliquid asset for a long period of time. A nonliquid asset is one that cannot be quickly and easily sold. Money that you have in a money market fund or a bank market rate account is totally liquid; that is, you can go to the bank at any time, withdraw your money, and have the cash in your hands. With a house, you can't do that.

Of course, you can always sell a house, but it can take time. In a bad market, you may not be able to sell for quite a while or for your desired price. This is one risk of ownership.

Further, since your money is invested in the house, it can't be invested in other, possibly lucrative, investments, such as mutual funds, stocks, etc. And the cash that you had to lay out for your down payment is no longer earning regular interest or dividends for you from bank deposits or other investments.

Upkeep

In addition to the regular costs of taxes, mortgage payments and utilities, you will also have periodic costs of repairs, maintenance and upkeep of your property. These can be costly and, if several problems arise at the same time (you could need a new roof and a new furnace during the same winter), it could spell economic disaster.

Equity

But owning and creating equity in your home will improve your credit rating and borrowing power. Your equity in your home is the total value of the home, less the principal amount owed on the mortgage and the amount of any other claims against the property. As you make your monthly mortgage payments, you pay both interest on your mortgage loan plus a part of the principal. This reduction of principal is called amortization. As you continue to pay off your mortgage, and the principal diminishes, each payment includes less and less interest and more and more principal. Your equity may build slowly at first but more rapidly later on. After you have finished paying off the mortgage and you own your house free and clear, it is said that you have 100% equity in the house.

With ownership, and an improved credit rating, you can use the equity you have in the house to borrow more money. Let's say that you want to borrow for your child's college tuition. You can do that by refinancing your mortgage so that you are borrowing more, or by taking a second mortgage on the house based on the equity you have in it. (Interest on such additional borrowings may not be fully tax-deductible—see the No Nonsense Real Estate Guide, *Refinancing Your Mortgage*. For a full discussion of real estate tax rules, see the No Nonsense Financial Guide, *The New Tax Law and What it Means to You*.)

5

THE DECISION TO BUY

So, the important thing to do, *before* you make your decision to buy, is to *think*. Think about your weekly expenses. Think about the big expenses that will come due within the next few years, such as college tuition. Consider the stability and regularity of your income.

Buying vs. Renting

Look carefully at the differences between buying and renting. Buying, as we said, affords you the pride of ownership, but it takes away your mobility because a house is sometimes hard to sell. Also, when you have invested time and money in fixing up a property you own, so that it is exactly to your liking, it's hard to leave it. If you anticipate changing jobs or having to move because of your job, ownership may not give you the mobility you need.

You don't pay for maintenance or upkeep if you rent, and you don't have to be your own janitor, or hire an electrician or plumber if something goes wrong.

Prepare a Budget

The first step in making your decision is to prepare your own budget or "cash flow" statement. This will give you an idea of the amount you can spend each month for housing. Once you know what you can spend, you can determine what type of housing suits you best.

There are many different ways of setting up a household budget or cash flow statement. We like a simple

18

3-column set-up, with one column for annual totals, and columns for weekly and monthly figures. The annual column must be filled in for each category; the weekly and monthly columns are to be used whenever convenient, both to let you see clearly how much you are spending and to arrive at the annual totals. A sample might look something like the example in Table 1 (we're assuming that you're not presently a home owner).

It's an easy form to use. For some items, like auto insurance and vacations, you'll probably find it easiest simply to put in annual totals. For items that you usually think of in terms of weekly totals, such as food, put in the weekly figure and multiply by 52 to get the annual figure; for items that are usually paid monthly, such as rent, enter the monthly figure and multiply by 12.

Now, using a similar sheet if you wish, calculate your expected monthly and annual costs of owning a house. Remember that as a home owner, you will have to spend not only for a mortgage, but also for utilities,

Household budget or cash flow statement

	Weekly	*Monthly*	*Annual*
Housing			
Rent	$	$ 400	$ 4,800
Elec. & Gas		80	960
Total		480	5,760
Other			
Food	100		5,200
Household	20		1,040
Meals Out	35		1,820
Entertainment	20		1,040
Clothing		100	1,200
Vacations			1,500
Gasoline			
Auto Insurance			
Life Insurance			
Tuition			
Etc., etc . . .			

maintenance and repair, home insurance, and property taxes.

On the other hand, you will save on federal (and possibly on state) income taxes because generally you can deduct the *interest* payments on your mortgage loan and the amount you pay in property taxes.

Assuming that the interest component of your payments is $800 per month, your property taxes amount to $400 per month, and you are in a 28% tax bracket, your annual tax saving would be:

$$(12) \times (\$800 + \$400) \times (.28) = \$4,032.$$

Now, consider the *down payment* that you will have to make in buying a house. Once you have done some shopping, you will know the price range in your area for the type of home you want to buy, how much of the total price can be covered by a mortgage loan, and how much will remain that has to be covered by you in cash at the outset (the down payment).

To the down payment, you should add the amount of upfront cash you will have to spend for closing costs, attorney's fees, and your costs of relocating, including moving costs, new furniture, etc. If you don't have that amount of cash available, you will need to figure how much you can save per month and how long it will take you to build up the necessary sum.

Now take a hard look at all the above figures. Assuming that you can manage the down payment, can you also manage whatever increase in monthly costs is involved in becoming a home owner? If not, can you see ways to save on other expenses?

If you are now managing to save regularly every month, would you be willing to save less in cash, and to put part or all of your saving effort into paying off a mortgage loan and in this way building up your ownership in your own home? A home may be as good an investment as you can find. But you may have to forego the flexibility and comfort that come from building up a cash reserve that you can get at quickly and easily.

Deciding whether to rent or buy is both a lifestyle decision and a financial decision.

Psychologically, ownership of your own house is a gratifying source of pride and security. Knowing that once your mortgage or other loan is paid off, you will be able to live in your own home forever, is a comforting fulfillment of the American dream.

While the American dream may not be all that it used to be, the financial advantages of owning a home are still very great. The tax advantages have been illustrated above. Moreover, we live in an inflationary world. If inflation continues, and it's hard to imagine otherwise, your home will usually appreciate in value. It is a nest egg to pass on to your children. For most people, buying a home is the best financial investment they will ever make.

6

AN INTRODUCTION TO HOUSE BUYING

What do you actually buy when you purchase a house? That depends on the documents you sign and the type of property.

Fee Simple Absolute

When you buy, you will usually purchase in *"fee."* Fee is an ancient British legal term that describes a form of ownership known, in full, as *"fee simple absolute."* In the United States, as well as in England, when you purchase a property in fee simple absolute, you purchase the entire parcel, the house, the land, and usually the air rights, forever and absolutely, with no doubts or questions possible about your ownership. Purchasing in fee allows you,to own, use and enjoy the land, without limitations (other than those specifically explained in the deed). Also, you can sell, give or will the land to whomever you wish. It is the most complete form of ownership that our law allows, and you should always make sure that your purchase is in fee.

Long-Term Leases

What other forms of ownership are there? We prefer to call some of them quasi-ownership, because your ownership is not complete. For example, you can purchase a long-term lease. This type of ownership is more common today in England than in the United States, but it is still of interest. When one of your authors lived in Cambridge, England, in the late 1960s, she lived in a portion of a large house which was owned by a lovely 86 year-old woman. This house was owned by her family on a 99-year lease, due to expire in the year 2010. You have no idea of the distress experienced the my landlady, who had no idea where she would move (at age 125, more or less) after her lease expired!

Lease-Purchase

Another form of quasi-ownership involves a lease-purchase, often called a lease with an option to purchase. This is a contractual arrangement which operates like a rental lease coupled with an agreement of sale. With a lease-purchase, you rent the house for a specified period of time, and have an option to buy it later at a given price. This arrangement allows you to "try out" the house for a while, and to lock in a purchase price in the beginning. Very often, the rent you pay during the lease portion of the arrangement, or a portion of it, is applied to the agreed-upon purchase price.

Rent With an Option to Purchase

Another arrangement is to rent with the option to purchase. This is similar to a lease-purchase, except that the purchase price usually is *not* predetermined, and has to be negotiated at a later date. The option keeps the seller from selling the property to anyone else during the term of your option. But later negotiations are advantageous to the seller because he or she knows that you are interested in the house, that you are settled in it, and that you want to stay. Be careful of this arrangement, because the price could go up.

Condominiums

You might decide that an individual house is not for you, and that you would like the maintenance-free shared-space living of a co-operative or condominium.

Buying a condominium (or "condo") is similar to buying a house, in that you buy your unit in fee. It is dissimilar because, in a condo, you also own an undivided pro rata portion of the common areas (lobby, halls, gardens, swimming pool, elevator, etc.) in conjunction with the other condo owners. This means that in addition to your monthly mortgage payments, you must pay a monthly maintenance fee to cover your portion of the upkeep of the common areas.

With a condo, you don't have the same amount of privacy and autonomy as in your own house. You have to live by the condominium rules, and they may be very strict, governing such matters as pets, children, etc. The rules also govern the use of common areas. You don't have the liberty to build a swimming pool or garden in your yard, because you don't actually own your yard—you share in the common area owned collectively by all the condominium owners.

One advantage of a condo is that you are relieved of the chore of maintenance of the common areas—the grounds, halls, lobby, etc. It is this maintenance-free way of life that many people appreciate. Service employees shovel the snow and do the gardening. Of course, you pay for these services in your monthly fee, but that is all part of the condo way of living.

Co-operatives

A co-operative (or "co-op") is a corporation which holds fee simple title to the co-op property. People purchase shares in the corporation and, in exchange, each shareholder receives a proprietary lease which allows him or her to occupy a specific unit within the property for as long as they own the shares.

Unlike the condo structure, a shareholder does not actually hold title to his or her unit, nor can a shareholder mortgage his or her shares. The co-operative corporation usually obtains a mortgage loan on the whole property but, if an individual needs to borrow money to finance his or her purchase, the financing is in the form of a personal loan. Each month, a co-op owner pays a fee which includes a pro rata portion of the corporation's mortgage payments plus maintenance costs for upkeep of common areas, and, in addition, the co-op owner must pay off any personal loan that he or she has taken.

Because you don't actually own your co-op unit, as you do with a condo, you are more limited in the things that you can do with it. In fact, in order to make changes in your unit, you will probably have to get the approval of the co-op board of directors.

Co-ops and condos have their advantages in joint ownership and shared responsibility and freedom from maintenance. But they also have negatives such as limitations on your right to alter and change your unit, and rules regarding the use of common areas. For more information on condos and co-ops, see the No Nonsense Real Estate Guide, *Understanding Condominiums and Co-ops.*

Who Is the Owner?

When one person buys a property, that person owns it in his or her own right and only one name appears on the deed.

The situation is different when two or more people want to purchase a property together. When a married couple buy a property, they usually own it as tenants by the entireties.

Tenants By The Entireties

This is a term carried over from England which signifies the ownership of property between a husband and wife. It means that each of the married partners owns the entire property, and, should one or the other die, the survivor will own it outright.

Joint Tenants with Right of Survivorship

This is similar to a tenancy by the entireties, except that the parties are not necessarily married and there may be any number of joint tenants. As with tenants by the entireties, the last surviving joint tenant ends up owning the entire property.

Tenants in Common

In this type of ownership, the owners each own a particular share of the property, but they have the right to use and enjoy the entire property. The shares remain legally separate; each can will, sell or otherwise devise his or her share, and the last survivor does not end up owning the whole.

Who Can Own Property?

As mentioned, married couples, friends or even perfect strangers can own property together. In addition to natural persons owning property, partnerships, corporations and trusts may also own property.

7

LOCATION, LOCATION, LOCATION

Once you have decided to buy a house, you have to make some very serious decisions. The first is determining where you want and can afford to live.

Builders, brokers, agents, and real estate experts all agree on one thing: the first and most important consideration in the home-buying decision is where to buy, or to use the common phrase—location, location, location.

How do you decide what neighborhood to choose? The best way is to ask. Ask friends who live nearby. Ask your relatives. Ask your priest, minister or rabbi for the name of someone who lives in the area. Ask people where you work. If the people who live in the area are your kind of people, then it should be a good neighborhood for you.

Schools

Even if you don't have or anticipate having children, you should check the schools. High quality schools are an important factor in the resalability of a house. If you have children, you will even more certainly want to make sure that the schools are excellent. If you are interested in private or parochial schools, make sure that they are available.

Look Around

Go to a church or synagogue. Look around. Do you feel comfortable? Take a drive through the area on a Saturday or Sunday. Look at the ages of the families. Do they have young children? Are there places for children to play? Do you want to be in an area away from children?

Look at the people who live in the area. Check the conditions of their homes. The condition of a neighborhood is very important, should you want to sell your home in the future. Go to shopping malls and the local stores. Look around. Strike up conversations over the fresh vegetables. Is the shopping convenient? Is the quality and quantity available and adequate? Check first and get to know your neighbors.

Find out what neighborhood organizations exist. Attend meetings. Meet people and get to know the area before you buy. If all this sounds time-consuming, remember that buying a house is too expensive and important a decision to be made casually.

At the same time, check the newspaper advertisements. Look for ads in the neighborhoods that interest you and see the prices of the homes. Are they within your range?

Long-Distance Purchase

Probably the most difficult task is to buy a house long-distance. Let's say that you have been transferred in your job and need to move quickly to a new area. We suggest that the best idea is to store your furniture for a time (this is usually not too expensive) and rent an apartment or a house until you get to know your new city. Jumping directly into purchasing before you really get to know a new area can be disastrous, even if you rely on information from people you think you can trust. There is no substitute for seeing for yourself. Avoid getting saddled with a house in an area that may not be right for you, just because you want to make a move quickly.

Rent for a While

The idea of renting while trying out an area can also be considered even if you are familiar with the area. Perhaps you want to try out a new part of town by renting before you decide to buy. In this case, a lease-purchase arrangement (see Chapter 6) might be ideal.

The important thing to remember is to take your time and think. The home you are looking for may be the biggest purchase of your life.

8

OLD HOUSE OR NEW HOUSE

An old house is any house that has had a previous owner. This is not necessarily a disadvantage, but it does mean that you had better check all the details of the house carefully before you buy.

Advantages of Old Houses

The first thing to keep in mind is that there are more old houses available than new houses. As a result, old houses tend to be less expensive than comparable new houses. And, because old houses tend to be in more stable and established neighborhoods, you can be more sure of where you are moving, the kind of people who live there, and the way the neighborhood will look a few years hence.

The location of older houses is often better regarding churches, schools, shopping and other services. And the landscaping of older trees and shrubbery will appear more lush and full. So older neighborhoods often tend to look more attractive and less barren than newer ones.

Older houses, especially if they were not tract houses to begin with, have an individuality that comes from previous owners who have made their own personal additions to them.

Many people believe that the construction of old houses is superior. And there certainly are amenities in older houses that would cost you dearly in new construction. Examples are hardwood floors, thicker wet plaster walls, expensive doorknobs and fittings, and copper rather than plastic pipes.

Disadvantages of Old Houses

The first and most important disadvantage of an older house is that you must be careful. You don't want to purchase someone else's old problem when you buy a used house.

Also, when you buy an old house, you have less chance of being able to customize your house inexpensively, as you often can with new construction.

Other disadvantages of old houses will be seen as we describe the advantages of new houses.

Advantages of New Houses

New houses tend to be better insulated and more energy-efficient than their older counterparts. Heat pumps and other energy-saving equipment are common in new construction. The wiring is often better, and new homes are built with an eye toward fire safety, with smoke and fire detectors built in. New homes tend to be more maintenance-free than older ones.

Property taxes in newer neighborhoods are often lower. Streets and public areas are of newer, more safety-oriented design than in older neighborhoods.

Modern construction brings with it modern facilities such as master bedroom suites, spacious closets, luxury bathrooms, and modern kitchens with new appliances. Recreational facilities are often built near new communities by builders who want to provide an appealing lifestyle to potential buyers.

And finally, but perhaps most importantly, new houses often come with warranties which provide a guarantee against structural and workmanship defects.

Disadvantages of New Houses

New houses, however, often look as if they have come off the assembly line. New housing often takes the form of "tract" houses, that is, cookie cutter style, with only 3 or 4 varieties to choose from. And new landscaping can make the area look even more barren.

New houses tend to be built on smaller lots, so that

you actually own less ground. And new houses tend to be in areas that are a greater distance from the center of things. Perhaps you will have a long commute to work, or will have to travel a distance for shopping until your area becomes more populated and merchants establish themselves there.

The single biggest complaint about new houses is that workmanship "isn't like it used to be." This may be true in some respects, but not in others. While you may not get extensive stone or carpentry detailing in a new house, your electric wiring, plumbing and drainage will not be like they used to be—they'll almost certainly be better.

The inability to get the builder to make repairs in the house and to put it in first class working order for you after you have settled can be the most important negative factor in a new house. We will learn how to solve this problem in Chapter 10.

9

THE NO NONSENSE
HOUSE-BUYING CHECK LIST

There are two difficulties that everyone encounters while house hunting. The first is to remember exactly what you want, including all the details. The second is to remember exactly what a particular house that you saw was like, after you have seen four, five or even ten houses in one exhausting day.

Because there are so many important and detailed items to remember, we have come up with a check list for you to fill out and take with you. You will find this list at the end of the book, after the Glossary.

We suggest that you photocopy the list and fill out one for each house you are interested in. Then, when you go home to think about what you saw, you will have an accurate record of all the details. One of the frustrations of house hunting is going home after a long day of seeing houses and having them all blend together into a fuzzy haze. Use your *No Nonsense Check List*. It may save your sanity. At least, if you are house hunting with a spouse or partner, it will save endless arguments about what you really saw.

10

WHAT TO LOOK FOR IN A NEW HOUSE

The most important thing to look for in a new house is the reputation of the builder. We have told you that the most important general principle in house hunting is location, location, location. Once you have found the right location for you, and decided on a new house, the rule becomes builder reputation, reputation, reputation.

Your new house is only as good as the person or company who built it. Check with people you know who have purchased and lived in other houses that this builder built. Are they happy? Are the houses sound? And, most important, were defects that were discovered *after* they moved in fixed promptly and with a minimum of aggravation?

Check the financial status of the builder. You will do well to ask your lender to do a credit check on the builder. A builder in shaky financial condition should always be avoided.

Check Builder Reputation

Don't necessarily take other people's word on builder excellence. Check for yourself. See as many of his or her houses as you can. Look around. Check for signs of sloppy workmanship, such as doors that don't close properly, rough edges, unfinished carpentry areas, or floors that aren't level. Check the outside landscaping. Are the houses holding up? Try and see a house built 10 years ago, or longer.

Talk to Other Owners

And, most important, talk to other owners, especially in the development you are interested in. Ask to actually look at their problem areas. Evaluate their complaints—are they reasonable? Is the house basically sound? Are their problems minor or serious?

National Association of Home Builders

Check with the Better Business Bureau for any complaints against the builder. And finally, check to see if the builder is a member of the National Association of Home Builders or another credible builders' association. While membership doesn't ensure excellence, it is one more way to check reputation.

Completion Date

Once you have determined that the builder has a good reputation and that his or her product meets your specifications, you should take time to consider the two most troublesome problems involved in buying a new house.

The first is that the house may not be completed on time. This sometimes happens, and it can be a particular problem if you have sold your previous house and need to move immediately into the new one. There are many reasons why a house may not be finished on time, and in many cases it is through no fault of the builder.

What can happen? Bad weather can preclude completion. Strikes can keep necessary materials from arriving on time. Bad weather in other parts of the country can prevent the receipt of goods.

But all that is irrelevant to you. You have no place to live. So, when settling on a new house, make sure that you leave some breathing room in planning the date when you move out of your present home. This will give you peace of mind and flexibility, should you need it. (For information on financing "bridge" or "swing" loans, see Chapter 15.)

Incomplete Work

The second common problem is incomplete work. This is the one single complaint most often heard from new home buyers. The reputation of your builder is the best guarantee that your house will be completed as you want. But there are other protections available for new house buyers.

Building Code

The first step you can and should take yourself. Find out under what building code your house is being constructed. In most parts of the country, it is the Building Officials & Code Administrators Code, known as the BOCA Basic Code. The Building Officials & Code Administrators International, Inc. is a nonprofit organization founded in 1915 to promulgate code rules for the construction trades. It is located at 17926 South Halsted Street, Homewood, Illinois 60430.

Once you know under what code (or under what specific modification of a code) your house is being constructed, you should hire an architect to periodically inspect your house during the construction phase.

The architect should also inspect the building plans and make specific recommendations for changes or additions relating to heating, appliances, types of windows, plumbing, etc. These recommendations, plus a right of periodic inspection by you or your representative, should then be incorporated in the agreement of sale.

Architect Inspections

Your architect should visit the house periodically and check to make sure that the builder does all that is supposed to be done under the agreement of sale, the applicable code and good building practices.

For example, your house needs a certain size joist. The joist is the heavy timber that rests on the foundation and holds the house up. It is impossible to ascertain what size joist was used once the house is constructed.

This is an area of great concern because the builder can cheat here and no one will know. Except you, the purchaser. You will know because your house will shake and you will never be able to fix the problem.

In addition, you will want a certain size of studs to be used as well as good quality timber, as specified in the BOCA or other applicable code. You won't be able to check these items yourself unless you are in the building business. That is why it is such a good idea to hire an architect to be your eyes and ears. And don't forget to have the architect inspect on a day after a good, solid rain, to check for a leaky basement.

Architect Fee

How much will your architect charge? Perhaps $100 per hour. How many times will the architect have to inspect the house? Perhaps five times. Adding perhaps one hour's travel time to and from the house for each inspection, this should amount to about 10 hours of work, or a cost to you of perhaps $1,000. In relation to the total cost of the house, this fee will be well worth it to you as a way of getting quality assurance, making sure that your detailed instructions are being followed, and giving you security and peace of mind.

Termite Certification

You have an advantage in a new house because it can be termite-proofed during construction. A termite shield can and should be installed in all new houses. And make sure that you get a termite certificate from the builder, warranting the construction against termite infestation.

Punch List

You and your architect should schedule a major inspection of the house several weeks before settlement. The architect will spot problems that you would not notice until you had lived in the house for 6 or 8 months. It is also a good idea to take your attorney with you, as any defects will have to be legally documented.

During this pre-settlement inspection, you will make what is called a "punch list." This is a list of defects and problems, drawn up by you and your representatives and signed and dated by the builder or builder's representative. The purpose of the inspection several weeks before settlement is to give the builder time to correct the defects you have noted.

Then, just before settlement, you and your representatives should inspect the house once again to make sure that the punched items have been corrected.

Settlement, Escrow, and Your Builder

What do you do if there are outstanding items that have not been corrected and you must go to settlement immediately? Of course, you can refuse to settle until all the items are completed. But this isn't practical if you have already sold your previous home and you need a place to live. And it may not be necessary if the items are details that you can live with, and you have some assurance that they will be promptly completed.

One solution is to *escrow* a portion of the settlement money in contemplation of completion. Under this arrangement, a certain portion of the purchase price is withheld from the builder until you are satisfied that all items have been finished. Your real estate attorney will know how to work out such an arrangement. The attorney can act as the escrow agent to hold the agreed-upon portion of the money in safekeeping until all the details have been completed; or it can be the title company, or another who is agreeable to all parties.

Some builders, however, will not accept escrow. Another way to handle the problem is to sign an additional agreement that the work will be done within a certain period—such as 30 days. You will need an attorney to handle the details here.

Such an agreement gives you less protection than an escrow arrangement. So you may have to make a hard decision. If the problem is major, you will not want to go to settlement anyway. But for smaller items, if the builder absolutely will not accept escrow, what do you do? The first thing is to analyze the item. Is it small? Is it something like the failure of the builder to install agreed-upon shrubbery because it is January and the ground is frozen? In that case, you have to rely on the reputation and honesty of the builder. And you must ask yourself the question, "What if this item *never* gets fixed?" How much money would it cost to fix it? How serious is the problem?

And finally, you must realize that no matter how many times you inspect the property, and no matter how many experts come with you, something will come up later that is unforeseen and that has to be fixed.

That brings us back to our first principle—*know your builder*. Know the builder's reputation for reliability. And remember that a builder's reputation is made with each house he or she completes. If your house has uncured problems and you tell others, it will be harder for the builder to sell the next house.

A builder friend of ours said, "My best advertisement is a satisfied customer." Not a completely original motto; but try to buy only from a builder who believes in it.

When the builder or builder's representative or superintendent does come back to repair something, don't pick that moment to take out your frustrations. It's almost always better to be nice. A good attitude will get more accomplished than threats or fights. Let your attorney threaten and fight for you. That's what attorneys are for. As a last resort, you can always threaten to tell your local newspaper about the problem. But be prepared actually to carry out the threat if it is made. And remember, you will only look foolish if you complain about something trivial; going public only works for real problems.

Warranty

One of the major advantages you have as the purchaser of a new house is a warranty. A warranty is a protection plan for the repair or replacement of defective merchandise or workmanship. What can get warranted? Just about everything. Make sure that you *read and understand all warranties completely.*

In a new house, all your appliances will come with warranties. And your entire house may have a warranty obtained by the builder.

Builder Warranties

Most new homes come with a warranty. Be wary of an unwarranted new house. Some builders warrant their own construction, but the better warranties are purchased by the builder, for a cost of about $2.00 to $2.50 per $1,000 of sale price, from one of the independent companies in the field such as the Home Owners Warranty, the Builders Trust Warranty or the Home Buyers Warranty. The cost of the warranty will probably be passed on to you by the builder, but a good warranty is definitely worth the cost.

H.O.W. Warranty

The most well known new construction warranty is the Home Owners Warranty (HOW). This is an excellent warranty offering 10 years of protection. The HOW warranty is accepted by the FHA and VA, and it is usually assumable by subsequent buyers.

During the first two years of a HOW warranty, the builder is responsible for repairing any major structural defects as well as any defects resulting from poor workmanship or materials. If the builder refuses to repair a problem, or if the repair is not done properly, a HOW arbitrator will be called in. The arbitrator's decision is binding on the builder. However, if the homeowner does not like the decision, he or she still has the right to go into court and sue the builder.

If you are not satisfied with the builder's performance in making required repairs, HOW has a grievance procedure to handle complaints quickly and professionally. If your house has a HOW warranty, make sure that you understand this procedure thoroughly before you buy the house, and that you follow it exactly, if needed.

In years 3 to 10, HOW warrants the house against major structural defects. All complaints must be directed to HOW, which is responsible for fixing them.

11

WHAT TO LOOK FOR IN AN OLDER HOUSE

A builder friend of ours claims that when you buy an old house, you buy an old headache. Of course, as a builder of new houses, he is clearly prejudiced against older construction, and you shouldn't let his warning worry you out of buying an older house. But there are many unknowns in an older house, and it will be just as well if you are worried into taking some necessary precautions.

Hire an Inspector

How can you tell if an older house is structurally sound? There are two ways. First, in many areas there are inspection services, companies whose business it is to inspect a house from top to bottom for a modest fee (usually $150 to $300). An inspection service gives you a written or oral report, covering as many details as you wish. Obviously, with a purchase as expensive as a house, spending a few hundred dollars more to ensure that the roof, foundation, wiring and plumbing are sound and that you are not buying an old headache is well worth the extra expense.

The American Society of Home Inspectors has a list of members. You can get a copy by writing to them at Suite 320, 655 15th Street, N.W., Washington, D.C. 20005.

Hire a Structural Engineer

Second, if you are in area where such inspection services don't exist, you can hire a structural engineer or an architect to inspect the house for you. We recommend the particular expertise of the structural engineer over the architect, but the choice is up to you. It's important to choose someone you trust.

Should you have a friend or relative who "knows houses" check the house? Here you may have a diplomatic problem. You should, of course, have them in and let them check around and knock on the walls all they wish. But unless they are professionally qualified, we strongly urge that you spend the relatively small amount needed for a thoroughly professional opinion.

Get Copies of Bills

One advantage of an older house is that it is easier to see the actual costs of running the house. The real estate agent or the owner of the house should supply you with copies of utility and tax bills. And it is better to see the actual bills than to take someone's word as to what the amounts are.

Utility Bills and Contracts

Make a point of finding out if any utility bills are paid on contract. A contract means that the gas, oil, or other utility company will take your average yearly consumption of their product and pro-rate payment for it over a twelve-month period. Under the contract system, you pay fixed amounts each month, rather than huge amounts in the cold winter months for heating and zero in the summer. Make sure that if there is no such contract, you see bills from all four seasons.

You should also ask if there are existing contracts for service on any included appliances, and ask to see copies of those.

Termite Certification

You should not buy an older house without requiring the seller to provide you with a certificate and warranty from a reliable inspection service guaranteeing that the property is free from termite infestation, and that any damage from previous infestations has been corrected.

Tax History

It is essential that you check the tax history of the property. In order to do this, you should check the current amount of taxes due each year and also find out when taxes were last raised. If possible, talk to a local attorney, accountant or politician and try to find out when taxes are likely to be raised again.

12

SUBMITTING AN OFFER

Once you have found THE house, what do you do?

The time has come to negotiate price. If you think you can do this for yourself—then go ahead. But we suggest that negotiations are often best handled by professionals and that a good real estate attorney will be able to negotiate a better deal for you. In the real estate market, deals are flexible and the range of possibilities is very wide, so that a good negotiator is the key.

Make an Offer

Remember that the seller's asking price is just that, an asking price. You don't know how much the seller really expects to get, and you can bid as far below the asking price as you think reasonable. So, make a bid. The worst that can happen is that it will be turned down. Once that happens, you can always make another, higher bid.

It is best to negotiate from a position of strength. If there are legitimate details about the house that need correcting, you should have found them out by now, and you should use them as leverage to reduce the price.

Using the Real Estate Agent

Use the real estate agent with caution. Remember that he or she is working for and being paid by the seller. Never tell the agent the absolute maximum you are willing to spend. That amounts to giving away your trump card before the game begins.

Submitting Bids on New Houses

You should be aware that the prices of new houses are negotiable, too. This is something you will rarely be told. Often, a builder needs to sell those first difficult houses immediately, in order for the rest of his or her financing to fall into place. This is a perfect time to make a low offer. If the builder remains firm on the price, try to have some desirable extras thrown in for free.

The Agreement of Sale

Once your offer has been accepted, it is time to write the details of the purchase in the agreement of sale. The contents of the agreement will be discussed in Part 4, Chapter 21.

13

ESCROW AND HOW TO HANDLE IT

Escrow is the holding by an impartial party of money deposited until certain conditions are met. In the case of the sale of a house, the escrow consists of the good faith deposit (also called the "earnest money") that the buyer makes to seal the deal.

Specifically, when you make an offer on a house, you propose a price at which you will buy, subject to the execution by both parties of an agreement of sale. You back up your proposal with a binder deposit—usually $500 or $1,000. If your offer is accepted, a final agreement of sale is drawn up with every detail included. After the offer and acceptance and the final agreement should come a period during which the buyer has the right to have the house inspected by an inspection service or engineer, whomever the buyer selects. The result of this inspection may allow for the buyer to withdraw the offer, if the terms of the offer so provide.

Assuming all goes well, and the agreement of sale is signed, the buyer must then put up a good faith deposit of 10% (usually) of the sale price, by check or in cash. This money is *escrowed*—that is, held on deposit—by an escrow agent agreed upon by the buyer and seller until closing.

Who Holds the Escrow Money?

It is always best to have your representative in charge of the escrow money, because the person in charge is the one who releases the money once all the conditions are met. From the buyer's point of view, the best escrow agent is his or her attorney. Second best is to have the money held jointly by the buyer's and the seller's attorney. If the house is a new one, the seller's lending institution often handles the escrow. In some states, the real estate agent customarily holds the escrow. You may not have a choice, but, as we said, it's always best to have your own person control the escrow if you can.

The time between the signing of the agreement of sale and the actual settlement is usually 60 to 90 days, but it can be shorter, or longer, depending on the needs of the people involved. Who earns interest on the escrowed money? Unless state or local law or custom provide otherwise, the recipient of the escrow interest has to be spelled out in the agreement of sale and is open to negotiation. Since there is no clear standard, we know of many situations when the judgment of Solomon worked best and the escrow interest was split evenly between buyer and seller.

14

CALCULATING YOUR DOWN PAYMENT

When you buy a house, one of the critical decisions you must make is how much of the purchase price you will pay in cash (the down payment) and how much you will borrow (the mortgage loan).

Down Payments—Large and Small

There are two schools of thought regarding how large a down payment you should make.

Those who favor large down payments say that real estate is a marvelous investment and the sooner you own the property, the better. A large down payment gives you immediate equity, or financial ownership, in the property. A larger down payment may help you to qualify for a mortgage loan on better terms than what you might otherwise get, possibly at a lower interest rate. And obviously, a larger down payment will result in a smaller mortgage and lower monthly payments on the mortgage.

Those who favor small down payments are urging you, in effect, to take advantage of your status as a home owner to borrow more rather than less. They point out that the higher monthly payments are less of a burden than might appear, since, especially at the beginning, the payments are largely interest on the loan, and this is tax-deductible.

A small down payment obviously gives you more leverage (see Chapter 4). You have bought a large asset with relatively little cash. If you want to buy a house that is expensive relative to your available cash, you have no choice but to make a small down payment.

A small down payment lets you stay more liquid. Instead of having all your savings tied up in the house, you can keep part of your savings working for you in investments that produce income, such as bank accounts, stocks, or mutual funds. These assets are liquid—that is, they are readily available to you should you need them for expenses or emergencies—and the extra income may offset (or even more than offset) the higher mortgage payments. However, if you invest the money carelessly, you may wish that you had used it for a larger down payment instead.

We should point out that qualified purchasers often can obtain FHA mortgages with as little as a 3% down payment, and VA mortgages require no down payment at all. (See Chapter 15.)

The decision as to how large a down payment to make will ultimately depend on you and your individual financial needs. It is a good idea to ask the advice of your accountant before finally deciding just how much money to put down.

15

MORTGAGES

What Is a Mortgage?

We all use the word *mortgage* for convenience when in fact we are talking about a mortgage loan. The mortgage itself is not a loan, but a *pledge*. This makes sense once you understand how a mortgage actually works. When we speak about "getting a mortgage," we actually mean the *mortgage loan*. A bank or other lender lends you the money for your purchase and in return you give the lender a mortgage (pledge); you have pledged your property as security for the repayment of the loan, plus any interest that has accrued on it.

The lender then registers your pledge with the appropriate local authority in the form of a *lien*. A lien is a legal notice that if the property is sold or if you fail to repay on schedule, the lien holder (lender) has a legal means, called foreclosure, of taking possession of the property in order to be repaid the amount owed.

Once the loan plus the interest has been paid off, the lien is removed and the pledged property is yours free and clear.

Obtaining Financing

Who will help you in your quest for financing? Surprisingly, more people than you think.

Builder

If you want a new house, the builder will probably have arranged to have mortgage money available for qualified buyers. As with any mortgage loan, you will be asked to fill out a detailed financial disclosure statement. These forms are rather standard, and two are reproduced in Appendix A.

Seller

If you are buying an older house, the seller will sometimes take back a mortgage, or partially assist with the financing. This can be a favorable arrangement, but make sure that your attorney draws the document carefully.

Buy-down

The builder of a new house (or sometimes the seller of an older one, or the buyer himself or herself) may buy-down the mortgage for the buyer. This means that the builder will pay the lender the cash equivalent of one or several points of interest so that the buyer has a lower interest rate to pay on the mortgage loan.

A buy-down can be either permanent or temporary. In a permanent buy-down, the builder pays the cash equivalent of interest points for the life of the loan. More prevalent is the temporary buy-down where the interest is reduced for a specified number of years. A common scheme is to buy-down 3% in the first year of the mortgage, 2% in the second, and 1% in the third. This is an excellent deal for the buyer, who benefits directly from the reduction in mortgage payments.

Broker

If the seller is not interested in financing, the broker will often assist you in obtaining a mortgage loan. You should know that in most areas the broker receives a fee from the mortgage company in return for bringing in customers. This should not worry you, if you follow the next piece of advice to be sure that the deal you accept is the best one available.

Shop, Shop, Shop

Just as we have had rules in triplicate to govern our choice of house and builder, so there is a rule to be followed in obtaining a mortgage. The rule is shop, shop, shop.

Where to Shop

Go to as many commercial banks, savings and loans, credit unions and mortgage companies as you can before you sign on the dotted line. Even with a new house and mortgage money easily available, we recommend that you still shop around.

In addition to the banks and other institutions mentioned above, you might also go to a mortgage consultant and/or to one of the new computerized mortgage origination networks that are just developing.

Mortgage Consultant

A mortgage consultant processes your application for subscribing lenders. Theoretically, this allows your application to be viewed by many lenders at once. There is no fee to the buyer for their service, but you should always check around to make sure that the deal they offer you is the best available.

Computerized Mortgage Network

A computerized mortgage network offers processing plus speed. Your application data is fed into a computer terminal and a mortgage commitment can be received in as little as 30 minutes. Once again, we caution you to comparison shop before signing.

One good source of mortgage information is the mortgage reporting services that are available in many areas. They tell you where the mortgage money is, the interest rates being offered, and the qualifications you must meet for each listed lender. They can save you considerable legwork.

The advice to comparison shop for mortgage

terms is especially true at this time. It used to be that mortgages were relatively standard, with fixed rates and for a fixed period of time, usually 20 to 30 years. Now that banking has been deregulated to some degree, mortgages are no longer uniform, and very different rates and "deals" are available from different lenders. This "creativity" in the mortgage business has led to the development of many new types of mortgages. We will discuss certain of these briefly; but for more extensive information on mortgages, see the No Nonsense Real Estate Guide, *Understanding Mortgages*.

Adjustable-Rate Mortgage

The most important change has been the development of the adjustable-rate mortgage or ARM (called an adjustable mortgage loan or AML by some savings and loan associations). With an ARM, the interest rate you pay is adjusted periodically according to fluctuations in some standard interest rate index, such as the current rate on U.S. Treasury bills. An ARM makes you gamble on the trend of interest rates. If interest rates generally go down, you may end up paying less each month. But if rates go up, you will have to pay more.

Most ARMS have maximums (called "caps") on the amount by which the interest rate can be raised at each adjustment period, or over the whole life of the mortgage, or both. The caps may also be expressed as a maximum monthly payment figure. Obviously, the lower the caps, the better for the borrower.

Negative Amortization

One major problem with ARMs is the potential for "negative amortization." Amortization is the process of paying off the principal amount of your loan; negative amortization means that the process is going the wrong way. This problem arises when the interest rate goes up, but the monthly amount that the lender can goes up, but the monthly amount that the lender can charge the borrower doesn't cover the increase—most likely because of a payment cap.

Negative amortization takes place because your monthly payments don't cover the revised interest charges on your loan, and the amount by which the payments fall short is added to the principal of the loan. So, while you are making your payments, the amount of your debt actually *increases*. Not a good situation at all.

There are four principles to remember when dealing with ARMs:

1. The lower the maximum and minimum caps are, the better.
2. A cap on the interest rate (rather than on payments) will avoid the problem of negative amortization.
3. The less frequently the interest rate is adjusted, the better.
4. The more stable the chosen index is, and the less subject to fluctuations, the better.

Balloon Mortgage

A balloon mortgage starts out like a fixed-rate mortgage, with payments calculated as if the loan were to be paid off in 20 or 30 years. However, in a balloon mortgage you only make your payments for a specified time—3, 5 or 10 years—after which time the entire amount of the mortgage loan becomes due and owing.

This means that when the mortgage "balloons," you have to find refinancing somewhere, and that may come at a time when mortgage rates are unfavorable to the borrower.

Graduated Payment Mortgage (GPM)

A GPM is a popular type of mortgage with young people who expect their incomes to rise over the next few years. A GPM can be either a fixed-rate or an adjustable-rate mortgage loan. With a GPM, the amount you pay is graduated so that you pay less at the beginning of the loan, and more as the loan progresses.

You should be careful to understand how much you will eventually have to pay, and to be reasonably sure you will be able to afford it. In addition, GPMs may have a negative amortization period at the beginning that you should be aware of.

Growing Equity Mortgage (GEM)

With a GEM, your monthly payments increase each year by a specified amount, usually 7½%. The extra 7½% is applied directly against the principal you owe, so that your equity in the property increases at a faster rate.

Mortgage Insurance

Many lenders of non-government backed loans require the buyer to purchase private mortgage insurance (TMI). Private mortgage insurance should not be confused with mortgage *life* insurance, discussed later in this chapter. The purpose of private mortgage insurance is to guarantee that if you default on the mortgage payments, the lender will get back the full balance of the loan.

If your down payment is less than 10% of the cost of the house, your lender will almost certainly require you to get mortgage insurance. Insurance will also probably be required if your down payment is between 10% and 20%.

The largest writer of mortgage insurance is the Mortgage Guarantee Insurance Company, known as MGIC (pronounced "magic"). Mortgage insurance is also written by many other companies and is sometimes provided by the lender itself.

Mortgage insurance costs have remained rather steady over time, averaging about $5 for every $1,000 of first year coverage. Insurance companies have recently begun to petition state governments to allow them to raise rates. They cite the rise in defaults on ARMs resulting from climbing interest rates as the reason for requiring the rate increases.

Cancelling Mortgage Insurance

Most lenders require you to carry this insurance for the life of the mortgage loan. This is an unnecessary expense for a borrower whose equity in the house has increased and whose outstanding loan principal is small compared to the value of the property. Many mortgage lenders follow a theory that when the outstanding balance on the loan is less than 80% of the purchase price, or if the balance is less than 80% of a current acceptable appraised value, insurance can be cancelled.

How much will you save by cancelling insurance? It could be as much as $125 to $175 per year. So check the mortgage contract with your lender before signing and try to see that the insurance is required only for a limited period. It will be harder to cancel insurance in situations where the lender is also the insurer. Many lenders are self-insurers and are reluctant to cancel policies that are bringing them money.

Mortgage Life Insurance

Mortgage *life* insurance should not be confused with the private mortgage insurance discussed above. The purpose of mortgage life insurance is to guarantee that the mortgage can be paid off if you die. You may be required to take out such insurance as part of the financing deal.

Mortgage life insurance is usually a form of *decreasing term* life insurance—the simplest and cheapest life insurance, with no savings element or cash value, and with the coverage decreasing each year to match the remaining principal amount of your mortgage. Again, you may be required to carry this insurance for the life of the mortgage, and again, the lender doesn't really need this protection after the first few years.

Swing Loan

One final word about financing. You may run into a timing problem, where you are forced to settle on your new home before you close on your old one. If the proceeds from the sale of the old house provide your down payment on the new one, you could experience a cash flow problem.

The solution may be a "swing loan" (also known as a "bridge loan"). This is a short-term loan for the amount of the down payment, secured by the equity you have in your old house. The lender will often charge an application fee (about $150), but no points. Interest is usually 1% above the lender's prime, and you pay the interest only until you settle on your old house. Then the principal and the interest on the swing loan become due in full.

16

TITLE

Title to a property signifies possession of that property and conveys with it absolute control and ownership over the land and everything that is on the land, including houses, trees, air, etc. When you buy a house from someone, you are purchasing the seller's title to the property. It is vital to you that the seller have "good and marketable title," insurable at the standard rates, to the property. The deed is the written representation of title.

What Is "Marketable Title?"

A marketable title is one that is reasonably free from defects and that conveys the right to use, sell and enjoy the property without unreasonable restrictions on the purchaser. All sorts of defects exist in titles. That is why you need a title company or an attorney to search the title for you.

Title Defects

The defects may come in many different forms. What if your seller once went bankrupt, and the person to whom he or she owed money filed a lien or judgment (that is, a legal notice) on the property? This lien, which represents an obligation to pay the debt owed to the creditor, is a "cloud" on the title.

A cloud means that when you go to purchase the property, the person who registered the lien can claim a portion of the purchase price to satisfy his or her obligation. If the seller refuses to pay the debt, and the lien is not satisfied, and you purchase the property, then the obligation to pay the creditor becomes yours. This is because the obligation to pay runs with the land, and the land now belongs to you.

This is only one example of the many different kinds of problems you can have with title. These problems are usually called "encumbrances," because they cast a shadow, or a cloud, on the title and encumber its free marketability.

Researching the Title

What do you do? You hire someone to research the title for you, to make sure that all is well. In most states, the buyer goes to a title company which searches the title to the property and gives a full title report. In other states, the title search is called an Abstract of Title or an Attorney's Record Search, done by a specialized attorney and followed by an attorney's opinion as to the condition of the title.

What does the attorney or title company actually do? They go to the courthouse, or to the office where the records of deeds are kept, and they read the history of the property. If the property is in a very old neighborhood, such as the Society Hill section of Philadelphia, or the Beacon Hill section of Boston, the search could take them back to pre-Revolutionary times, because the ownership history of the property goes back that far. With a newer property, the history is much shorter, and, with a new development, the title work will have already been done by the builder, who bought the property prior to building on it.

Title Insurance

The result of the title abstract or search is contained in the opinion or report and is presented to the buyer at settlement. Despite this report, it is important for the buyer of any property to purchase title insurance. This is readily available and it insures the buyer that the title is good, clear and marketable, and that if any title problems arise, the title insurer will pay to have them cleared.

Title insurance can be purchased in every state, and, in almost every state, title insurers are regulated by state law. The fee for the insurance is a one-time charge. You might consider shopping around for title insurance, as the prices can vary and the services actually rendered for this one-time fee can also vary. Check for the best deal.

Deed

The deed is the actual legal document representing ownership (title) that is signed and transferred from seller to buyer and is recorded as an official document. The deed will also recite a survey of the property.

Survey

The survey in a deed is a verbal description, usually in rather archaic language, of the position and dimensions of the plot of land, the structures on the plot, and other relevant details. It will also include descriptions of easements and other additions to the land.

Easements

An easement is a legal right of way. For example, the electric company may have an easement to run wires or cable over or under your property. This type of easement usually doesn't hamper the marketability of the property.

There may, however, be easements recorded on the deed and reflected in the title search that you do not like. For example, suppose that one of your neighbors has an easement on your land so that he or she can cross your land to get to a public lake nearby. Let's say that this easement was recorded in 1900, before roads and sidewalks were built in your neighborhood. At present there is a perfectly good sidewalk path that your neighbor could use. Now let's say that you want to put a tennis court on your land, but the tennis court will have to be built on the part of the land covered by your neighbor's easement.

What do you do? First, you call your lawyer, because you know that if you build on your neighbor's easement, he or she could sue you. Then, negotiate with your neighbor to get the easement removed. You might have to make a cash payment, or even give your neighbor the right to use the tennis court, in exchange for removing the easement.

So any easement, like any encumbrance, restricts your absolute and total control over your property. Remember that you will rarely find an encumbrance-free property, and that most easements, such as those for electricity, sewage or telephone cable, are perfectly acceptable. However, you shouldn't make any commitments on a property without first checking to see if there are any unacceptable easements. This is another good reason for hiring a real estate lawyer.

17

INSURANCE

In addition to the title insurance, the buyer should immediately obtain homeowner's insurance on the property.

There are several types of homeowner's insurance. There are basic policies which protect primarily against fire and windstorm, and more extensive policies which protect against a wide range of hazards. Talk to your insurance agent about the coverage that you need. Make sure that your insurance includes personal liability coverage to protect you if anyone is injured on your property.

When To Buy Property Insurance

You should buy the insurance as soon as the agreement of sale is signed. Once it is signed, you become the "equitable owner" of the property. Then, if the house burns down, you will still be required to go to settlement and pay the full price, unless the agreement of sale provides otherwise.

PART III
SELLING A HOUSE

18

CLEAN-UP, FIX-UP, PAINT-UP

We now turn to the seller. The goal of the seller, of course, is to sell the property for as much money and as quickly as possible.

For better or worse, everyone is strongly influenced by appearance, and house buyers are no exception. The more attractive you can make your house, the easier it will be to sell and the quicker it will sell.

So, it is definitely worth spending the time and money needed to paint the house and spruce it up. The money you spend in this way is deductible for tax purposes in computing the profit from the sale of your house. Just what work to do is up to you—but we can definitely say that the more you do, the more desirable your house will become, and the better chance you will have of selling it for a higher price.

Exterior

The first thing to do is to go outside and look, *really look*, at your property. Does the lawn need mowing? Do the shrubs need trimming? Is the exterior paint and trim in good condition? Nothing can throw a potential buyer off the track more quickly than a shabby exterior because it signals two things: first, that the entire property is shabby and in need of repair; and second, that you, as the owner, haven't cared enough about your property to take care of it as it deserved.

So, take a good look, and in the month or so before you put the house up for sale—fix it up.

Interior

Next, go inside and look around. People are always interested in the size of the closets, and it's perfectly normal for a potential buyer to open your closets and look inside. Clean them. Remove clutter. Remember that a cluttered closet looks much smaller than a neat one. Even if you have to put some things in storage—it's well worth it.

Does the interior need paint? You have no idea how much one coat of white or off-white paint will do for a house. First, it opens up the rooms visually, making them appear brighter, sunnier and airier. Second, new paint indicates a degree of care that is psychologically appealing to a buyer.

Rugs should be cleaned (good do-it-yourself spray cleaners are easy and inexpensive). Windows, kitchen cabinets, and bathrooms should be spotless.

Valuables

Now, for a word about valuables. You might consider removing valuable art objects and jewelry from your house for the period when it is being shown to large numbers of people. Not all people who look at houses are buyers, and it is well known that potential burglars can pose as buyers to "case the house." So, valuables are better off stored or put in safe deposit for the duration.

Light Up

It is also a good idea to turn all the lights on in the house before anyone comes in to look at it. Keep the shades up (unless you are hiding an unsightly view) and try to make the place look as bright, cheerful and happy as possible.

Pets

If you have an animal, try to get all odors out of the house. People who are animal haters or allergic will be turned off by animal smells. And it also helps to keep your pet outside, if possible, when potential buyers call. Many people are afraid of animals, and you don't want a potential buyer upset.

19

TO BROKER OR NOT TO BROKER IS OFTEN THE QUESTION

Using the services of a real estate broker and his or her staff is both a convenience and an expense. It is a convenience because the broker takes care of advertising the house, screening customers, and showing it to potential buyers. The broker will also usually be instrumental in helping the buyer obtain a mortgage.

You, the seller, must pay the broker's commission—typically 6% of the sales price. The 6% is a rough national average for sales commissions to brokers on residential properties. You should check regarding the exact percentage charged by brokers in your area. If you discover discrepancies among the amounts charged, you should contact the local real estate board before you sign with any broker.

The table below shows broker fees at 5%, 6% and 7%.

Typical Broker's Fees

Sale Price	Fee at 5%	Fee at 6%	Fee at 7%
$30,000	$1,500	$1,800	$2,100
$50,000	$2,500	$3,000	$3,500
$75,000	$3,750	$4,500	$5,250
$100,000	$5,000	$6,000	$7,000
$125,000	$6,250	$7,500	$8,750

But using a broker may not really cost as much as appears from the fee schedule. Often, the price of the house is adjusted to include the broker's commission. In addition, a broker will pay some of the costs that you would have to pay if you were selling the house yourself, such as newspaper advertising and the sign for your front porch or lawn. Using a broker makes your life easier. You are spared the time and aggravation of speaking to many callers on the phone. (And, without someone to screen them, you don't know whether these callers can afford to buy your house, even assuming that they like it.)

With a broker, there are no surprise visits by strangers to see your house at odd hours. Brokers make appointments at your convenience.

We admit to a prejudice in favor of the convenience and security of having a broker on your side. But should you try to go it alone, here are some tips.

Selling Without a Broker—Pricing

Brokers are familiar with the prices of comparable houses in your area and are qualified to set a reasonable price for your house. But you can pay for a price estimate by hiring a professional appraiser, which usually costs between $150 and $300. Or, you can begin the whole procedure by calling several brokers and asking for opinions as to the price at which your house might sell. This will give you guidance as to your asking price—which you can set higher or lower, depending on how anxious you are to sell quickly. Also, in this way you will have already interviewed brokers, should you later decide to engage one.

The Broker's Contract

If you do decide to hire a broker, we recommend that you have a written agreement and that your attorney look it over and explain it to you before you sign. In most states, oral agreements regarding land are not binding, and the broker needs the contract more than you do. But you should be careful and commit your arrangement to writing, just in case of dispute.

The contract must contain certain features, among them, the location of the house, what contents are included, if any, the exact price, the amount of commission (expressed as a percentage), and the period of time that the contract will last. We suggest that the shortest contract is the best one. Agents will feel that they have to move your house more aggressively if they only have 90 or 120 days to earn their commission.

Avoid the trap of having a clause in your agreement that allows the broker to earn a fee, for a certain period of time *after* the agreement is terminated, no matter who actually sells the house. However, as we shall see in a moment, it is not unusual for the broker to be in this "exclusive" position for the period over which the contract is effective.

Exclusive Right to Sell

There are several different ways to list your property with a broker. The most common is the exclusive right to sell. This gives the broker a commission regardless of who actually sells the property. Remember that, with this type of agreement, you will owe a commission even if you find the buyer and negotiate the sale yourself.

Exclusive Agency Listing

An exclusive agency listing is the same as the exclusive right to sell, except that it reserves in you the right to sell the property yourself without paying the broker's commission. It is rare that a broker will agree to this type of contract, and it often precludes you from being listed on the multiple listing service.

Open Listing

An open listing (also called a non-exclusive listing) is used in areas where no multiple listing service exists. In this arrangement, your house can be listed with several different brokers, and the one who actually makes the sale receives the commission. This arrangement also reserves your right to sell the house yourself without commission. This type of agreement does not give much incentive to any broker to really push your property.

Multiple Listing Service

The multiple listing service (MLS) is one of the happiest inventions of the real estate business. With it, every broker in your area who is a service member learns about the availability of your house and its features, and each has the opportunity to sell it.

A multiple listing therefore increases your chances of sale. All members of the MLS sign an agreement regarding the splitting of commissions, should a nonlisting broker (called a co-operating broker) make the sale.

It is important for you to find out whether multiple listings exist in your area, and if the broker you have selected is a service member. If so, you must then find out when your broker will list your house on the MLS. You might want to check with the local board of realtors and with the MLS itself to make sure that your broker lists your house as soon as possible.

What If You Are Dissatisfied with Your Broker?

Obviously, you should try to be sure of your broker before you sign. However, mistakes can happen; and if you find that your broker is not doing the type of job you want, or if your rapport is poor, you might want to change. It is because of this possibility that we advise signing the shortest possible agreement with the broker.

If you are extremely dissatisfied with your broker, you can go to the local board of realtors, who should have a grievance procedure for you to follow. This may be time consuming, however, and it will probably not do much for selling your house. A lawsuit is another time consuming possibility.

We suggest that you proceed carefully, read before you sign, and then sign a short-term agreement. This will give you the freedom to change brokers should that become necessary.

20

ANALYZING OFFERS

Here are the details of what happens when someone wants to make an offer for your house.

If you are using a broker, the buyer will go to the broker and make a firm offer. If you are selling your house yourself, the buyer comes directly to you. The broker will write down the offer and a take a good faith deposit of $500 or $1,000. The broker will give the buyer a receipt evidencing the deposit. Specified in the offer will be the offered price, the date of the offer, for how many days the offer will remain in effect, and the conditions that the buyer requests before the offer becomes binding.

Conditions

Conditions could include the negotiating of an agreement of sale acceptable to all parties and/or the right of the buyer to inspect the house. If any conditions are not met, the nonbinding offer will be withdrawn and the deposit refunded.

Your broker will report to you the details of the offer. You have the option of either acccepting the offer with its conditions, or negotiating, usually through the broker, for more money or more favorable conditions.

Negotiations

Brokers have several theories as to why you, the seller, should not hold out too long when negotiating real estate deals. The old wives tale is that your first offer is usually your best, and your first buyer will give you the best deal. This seems to have no logical basis, but we have heard it from many reliable realtors, and so we pass it on to you.

The second theory about accepting offers is the "bird in the hand" argument. Get the money now— why take chances that other buyers may never come along? Of course, you should not accept an outrageously low offer just because it is the only one you have in hand at the moment, but you should seriously consider offers that are within reason. Offers are better than dreams of offers.

You should also realize that while it may be very important to you to get the offer up by another $5,000 or so, it really is not that important to the broker. After all, to the broker another $5,000 on the price means additional time and effort and only an additional $300 in commission. This is a perfect time to use your attorney to negotiate the final sale price. A good real estate lawyer will know how to try for an extra $5,000, and when to settle for less.

If you are negotiating for yourself and you sense that you won't be able to get your asking price, you can always suggest ending the stand-off by splitting the difference. Let's say that you want to sell the house for $5,000 more than the buyer is offering to pay. If you can convince the buyer to raise his or her offer by $2,500 while you come down $2,500, it may be a good compromise for both parties.

PART IV
THE HAPPY ENDING

21

THE AGREEMENT OF SALE

The Agreement of Sale

The agreement of sale is a legal document that binds the buyer to purchase, and the seller to sell, a particular house. Because it is a legal document, and full of potential pitfalls, we strongly recommend that you engage a competent real estate attorney to draft the document for you.

Note that the agreement of sale doesn't yet make the buyer the actual owner of the house. That only happens at settlement. (See Chapter 22.) It is at settlement that the legal right to the property transfers from seller to buyer, who is then legally entitled to the keys. There are many pitfalls between agreement and settlement, and a good attorney can save you from much worry and possibly from major mistakes.

Choosing an Attorney

If you don't know an attorney who specializes in real estate, you can ask your own attorney for a recommendation. Or you can ask a friend who recently purchased a home, or call the local bar association. The bar association will have a list of qualified attorneys from whom you can choose.

You should make an appointment to interview any proposed attorney. Draw up a list of questions to ask, including questions about the lawyer's specific experience and qualifications in dealing with real estate matters. No one can be a specialist in everything, and a lawyer may be the best entertainment attorney or divorce attorney in the state, and still be completely un-qualified to help you when you are about to buy a house.

You should definitely ask about fees. You want to know as precisely as possible how much the attorney's services will cost you. Does the lawyer charge on an hourly basis, or is the fee a fixed one for the entire transaction? Does it sound reasonable to you? You might want to ask friends how much they paid their attorney in the same situation. Or you could call the local bar association and see if the fee you have been quoted is in line with local guidelines established for such transactions.

Remember that there are several areas in which you need the expertise of an attorney. First are the negotiations surrounding the agreement of sale. For a new house, there are the items on the punch list (see Chapter 10). For an older house, there are any items that the inspection service or structural engineer has found and the owner has agreed to fix before settle-ment. There are also the questions of the escrow money (see Chapter 13), and attendance at the settlement or closing (see Chapter 22). In light of the total cost of the house, the additional payment to an attorney to ensure that all goes well and in your favor is definitely worth-while.

It's unwise to have the same attorney represent both parties to a sale, even though the builder of a new house may offer you the services of his or her attorney for free. Think twice before accepting such an offer. If your interests are to be protected, your attorney should be working only for you.

Each Word Is Important

The agreement of sale, which defines the rights and obligations of the parties, is *the* most critical document in any real estate transaction. Each and every word in the agreement of sale is important *and* negotiable. Re-member that once you sign the agreement of sale, you are stuck with whatever it says—or doesn't say—about the transaction.

The following major items should appear in every agreement:

Parties

The names of the buyer and seller and any other persons who have an ownership interest in the property must be listed. In states where spouses may have an interest in real estate even if they are not the "record" owner, they should sign the agreement (and the deed, too).

Property

A precise description of the property is necessary. Both a street address (if there is one) and an exact "legal description" as recorded on public records are advisable.

Purchase Price

The price being paid for the property, in U.S. dollars, must be specified.

Payment Terms

The deposit to be made upon signing the agreement ("earnest money") and the additional amount to be paid at settlement must be stated.

Mortgage Contingency

If the buyer needs to obtain a mortgage loan to complete the purchase, the agreement should contain a carefully written mortgage contingency clause. This clause says that if the buyer does not obtain a mortgage commitment letter from a lender for a loan of a specified amount, at a stated interest rate and for a certain term (for example, a $50,000 loan at 10% for 30 years) within a definite number of days from the date of the agreement (for example, 45 days), the buyer has the right to call off the deal and have all of his or her earnest money returned.

This clause is important to both the buyer and the seller. Without it, the buyer would be obligated to purchase the property whether or not a mortgage loan was obtained, and the seller could sue for performance. The buyer would also forego the earnest money deposit. The seller gains by this clause because it forces mortgage lenders to make commitments promptly.

Zoning Clause

There should be a clause stating that the zoning classification of the property must be appropriate for the intended use by the buyer as a precondition of closing the sale.

Termite Inspection

The buyer should require the agreement to state that the sale is conditioned upon the property being inspected and pronounced free from infestation and damage from any prior infestations. The inspection should be backed up by a warranty for at least 2 years.

Building Inspections

The buyer ought to include the right to have the roof, walls, floors, plumbing, heating, electrical systems and any and all other parts of the property inspected by persons of the buyer's choosing.

The agreement should state that if such inspections result in reports of structural or systematic damage, or the need for repairs beyond a specified dollar amount, the buyer can cancel the agreement and have all deposit monies returned.

You should note that adverse reports usually result in an adjustment of the sale price. Without this clause, however, the buyer has no bargaining power to force such an adjustment.

Risk of Loss

The issue of risk of loss is a very important one to the buyer because failure to provide for the possibility may result in the worst of all possible results: the buyer having to pay full price for a property which has been destroyed. In most states, once the buyer executes the agreement of sale, the risk of loss to the property passes to him or her.

There are two ways to handle this. First, the buyer can purchase insurance on the property (see Chapter 17). Second, the agreement can be drafted to state either that the risk of loss remains with the seller and in the event of partial or total destruction the agreement is voided and the buyer gets his or her money back, or that the seller agrees to maintain the insurance in the amount of the sale price with the buyer as the "loss payee"—that is, the beneficiary of the policy. In that case, if the property is partially or totally destroyed, the buyer will have to settle on the property, but will receive the insurance money.

Nature of Title

Many people who sell property claim to use a "standard form" agreement of sale. These forms tend to favor the seller over the buyer and, in addition, are severely lacking in clarity when they describe the nature of title to be transferred from seller to buyer.

Form agreements often refer to the transfer of a "quitclaim deed," which means that the seller agrees to transfer whatever title the seller has in the property—no matter how defective or tainted it is. A "general warranty deed," on the other hand, carries with it greater assurance that the seller is transferring title that he or she agrees to defend, if necessary.

Key language to protect the buyer regarding title should read something like this:

Seller will at settlement transfer to buyer good and marketable title to the property, free and clear of any liens, encumbrances and easements except building restrictions, easements of roads or public utility companies or existing law, which title shall be insurable at regular rates by a reputable title insurance company.

Contents

In most states, "fixtures" are deemed to be part of the property and included in the purchase. Certain other items may be required to be included, such as stoves and lighting fixtures. In order to avoid problems, it is best to be specific in the agreement regarding these and any additional items (such as a built-in stereo system, Amana refrigerator, wall-to-wall carpeting in the living room, dining room chandelier, etc.) that are being purchased. If additional money is to be paid for any item, the sum due should be specified.

Timing and Possession

The agreement should clearly state the time by which settlement should occur. Both buyer and seller should negotiate a settlement date that meets their needs.

The agreement should state that the settlement date is the date of possession of the completely vacated property. The agreement should also say that if possession is to be delayed for any reason, the buyer may hold back a part of the sale price until after the seller vacates, to protect against damage, theft, or costs incurred as a result of the delay (such as additional rent, storage, etc.).

The property should be inspected the day of settlement to make sure that all is in order and physically present. Keys should be turned over to the buyer at settlement, and the buyer should immediately change the locks upon taking possession.

Escrow

The escrow agent should be identified. The money should be held in an interest-bearing bank account, and the agreement should state who receives the interest.

Broker's Commission

The amount of commission, and who must pay it, must be stated, as well as what happens if the sale doesn't conclude.

22

SETTLEMENT OR CLOSING THE DEAL

Everyone seems to approach settlement (also known as closing) with fear and trepidation. Things will go properly, however, if you follow these simple rules: do your homework and go well prepared.

What Is Settlement

Settlement is the time when the buyer becomes the actual owner of the property. Many documents are signed and much money changes hands.

Be Prepared

Bring extra checks with you, several pens, and a calculator to check the numbers. Bring all your documents with you and check the final papers against your preliminary drafts for any discrepancies. It is a good idea to take your attorney with you so that any problems that arise can be settled on the spot.

Good Faith Estimate

Within three days after application for a mortgage loan, the lender must supply the borrower with a good faith estimate of settlement charges. This is according to the federal Real Estate Settlement Procedures Act (RESPA). A copy of the standard RESPA form is reproduced in Appendix B.

The Settlement Sheet

The "settlement sheet" is a document prepared at the settlement, or closing, of a real estate purchase which details all the various charges paid to and by each party to the transaction. A sample of the HUD settlement sheet is reproduced in Appendix C.

Remember that there are different rules and customs relating to which party pays what settlement costs. You should check with your lender, attorney, and real estate agent to avoid any surprises.

There are often extra costs that might not show up on the good faith estimate. These can include taxes, title search fee, mortgage and title insurance, homeowner's insurance, prepayment of utilities, attorney's fees, and adjustments. In addition, there will probably be a mortgage loan origination fee. The lender is likely to charge between 1 and 4 points, or 1% to 4%. One percent is most common. These costs usually are paid by the buyer, but custom or agreement of the parties could allow for the seller to pay them, or for each of the parties to pay one-half. Many of these charges are expressed in terms of "points," each point representing 1% of the face value of the mortgage. So, if the mortgage loan were for $50,000, one point would cost $500.

CONCLUSION

Home owning is fun, excitement, hard work, comfort and security. We wish you joy and happiness in your new home.

GLOSSARY

Abstract of Title A record of the title, or history of owner-ship, of a property.

Adjustable Mortgage Loan (AML) Similar to an ARM, and offered by savings and loan associations. See Adjustable-Rate Mortgage.

Adjustable-Rate Mortgage (ARM) A mortgage whose inter-est rate is periodically adjusted according to an agreed-upon index.

Agreement of Sale The legal contract between the buyer and the seller of a property including the sale price, settlement date, and all conditions and terms of the sale.

Amortization The process by which the principal amount of a loan is reduced through periodic repayments.

Appraisal An expert evaluation of the fair market value of a property.

Appreciation An increase in value of a property.

Assumable Mortgage A mortgage that can be taken over on its original terms by a subsequent buyer of the house. All FHA and VA mortgages are assumable.

Attorney's Opinion of Title An Abstract of Title.

Attorney's Record Search and Opinion See Abstract of Title.

Balloon Mortgage A type of mortgage loan where monthly payments are made until a certain date when the re-maining balance due becomes payable in full.

Beneficial Owner See Equitable Owner.

Bridge Loan See Swing Loan.

Building Officials and Code Administrators International Code (BOCA Code) The building code used nationwide in most residential construction.

Buy-Down A procedure by which the seller or builder of a house permanently or temporarily reduces the amount of interest the buyer will have to pay by paying "points" to the mortgage lender at closing.

Buyer-Agent An agent hired and paid for by the buyer of a house to find the appropriate property and negotiate for its purchase.

Clear Title See Marketable Title.

Closing The time when legal title to a property passes from the seller to the buyer. Also termed Settlement.

Collateral The security for repayment of a loan. In a

mortgage loan, the property is pledged (mortgaged) as security.

Computerized Mortgage Networks   Organizations which originate mortgage loans through the use of computers.

Condominium (Condo)   A form of joint property ownership. Title to a specific condo unit is held in fee simple, with common elements jointly owned by all condo owners together.

Conventional Mortgage Loan   Any mortgage loan that does not have government backing.

Co-operating Broker or Agent   A broker or agent, other than the original listing broker, who actually sells a property when it is listed with the Multiple Listing Service.

Co-operative (Co-op)   A form of joint property ownership where the entire development is owned by a co-operative corporation whose shareholders have the right to occupy individual units.

Deed   The piece of paper filed according to law which evidences title (ownership) of a property.

Deed of Trust   A loan instrument used in some states in lieu of a mortgage.

Defect in Title   A problem with the title to a property which may render the title not marketable. Also termed "cloud" on title.

Down Payment   Cash payable by the buyer of a property equal to the difference between the total sale price and the amount of the mortgage loan.

Easement   The right to enter or use a portion of the land of another for a specific purpose.

Earnest Money   The deposit given by the buyer to the seller to show serious intent to purchase.

Encumbrance   Any claim, charge, lien or liability against a property.

Equitable Owner   The person who has signed an agreement of sale for a property but who does not as yet hold legal title to it.

Equity or Owner's Equity   The amount by which the present market value of a property exceeds the amount of the mortgage and all other debts, claims or liens against the property.

Escrow   Money deposited and held by a neutral party in contemplation of a purchase.

Exclusive Agency Listing   A contract with a real estate agent which reserves to the seller the right also to sell on his or her own, without paying a commission.

88

Exclusive Right to Sell A contract with a real estate agent giving the listing agent a commission regardless of who actually sells the property.

Federal Home Loan Mortgage Corporation (Freddie Mac) A quasi-governmental agency which purchases mortgages from the original mortgage lenders.

Federal Housing Authority (FHA) A part of the U.S. Department of Housing and Urban Development which offers mortgage loan insurance programs to buyers of qualifying properties.

Federal National Mortgage Association (Fannie Mae) A quasi-governmental agency, now publicly owned, which purchases mortgages from the original mortgage lenders.

Fee Simple Absolute (Fee) The best and most complete form of legal ownership, carrying the absolute right to use, sell, or bequeath property in any manner desired.

Foreclosure The legal remedy used by a mortgage lender to assume ownership of a property when required loan repayments are not made.

Good Faith Deposit See Earnest Money.

Government National Mortgage Association (Ginnie Mae) A quasi-governmental agency, carrying the full faith and credit of the United States government, which purchases mortgages from the original mortgage lender.

Graduated Payment Mortgage (GPM) A type of mortgage loan where the repayments start small and gradually increase.

Home Owners Warranty (HOM) One of the best 10-year warranties available for newly built houses.

HUD The U.S. Department of Housing and Urban Development.

Joint Tenants A form of property ownership between two or more persons with "right of survivorship," where all can use and enjoy the whole property, and on death the whole property is owned by the survivor(s).

Joist The heavy timber that carries the floor.

Lease Purchase An agreement whereby a person can rent a property for a certain period of time and then have the option of buying the property for a specified price. Often a portion of the rent paid is applied against the purchase price.

Leverage Using a small amount of money (capital) to obtain ownership and/or control of a large property.

Lien A legal notice, filed according to law, of the right of a lien holder (such as a mortgage lender) to be paid from the proceeds of the sale of property on which the lien was recorded.

Liquid Investment An investment that can be turned into cash easily and quickly.

Listing Broker or Agent The real estate broker or agent with whom a seller has listed his or her property.

Marketable Title Title to a property which renders the property free and clear and able to be transferred freely.

Mortgage The legal document representing a loan of money in return for the pledge of property as collateral for the repayment of the loan with interest.

Mortgage Commitment The written notice from a mortgage lender that your mortgage application has been approved and that for a specified time period the mortgage loan will be available for you to buy a specified property.

Mortgagee The person or company who receives the mortgage as a pledge for repayment of the loan. The mortgage lender.

Mortgagor The mortgage borrower who gives the mortgage as a pledge to repay.

Multiple Listing Service (MLS) A service where house listings of member real estate agents are made available for all agents to sell. Commissions from multiple listing sales are split between co-operating agents.

Negative Amortization The process of adding to the principal balance of a loan when current payments do not fully cover the required interest.

Non-Exclusive Listing See Open Listing.

Open Listing A contract with one or more real estate agents giving each the right to sell for a commission, but reserving to the seller the right to sell without commission.

Option to Purchase An agreement whereby a person pays for the right to buy a property for a specified time and at a specified price.

Origination Fee A fee, usually amounting to one to four points (1% to 4% of the amount of the mortgage loan), charged by a mortgage lender at the inception of the loan.

Points Charges levied by the mortgage lender and usually payable at closing. One point represents 1% of the face value of the mortgage loan.

Prepayment Penalty A charge imposed by a mortgage lender on a borrower who wants to pay off part or all of a mortgage loan in advance of schedule.

Principal   The face amount borrowed in a mortgage loan.

Punch List   A list compiled by the buyer on the pre-settlement inspection detailing all defects and problems found in the property. The list is signed by the buyer and co-signed by the builder or his or her representative.

Real Estate Agent   An employee of a real estate broker who has passed an examination and is licensed by the state.

Real Estate Broker   A person who has passed an advanced examination and is licensed by the state to show houses to potential buyers and to negotiate purchases and sales, and to receive fees for such services.

Realist   See Real Estate Broker.

Realtor   See Real Estate Broker.

Salesperson   See Real Estate Agent.

Settlement   See Closing.

Survey   A legally precise description of a property including the location and size of the land and all buildings thereon.

Swing Loan   A temporary loan obtained when you are buying one property before you sell another.

Tenants by the Entireties   The legal form of ownership of property jointly by husband and wife.

Tenants in Common   A form of property ownership where two or more persons own a property and all can use or enjoy it and each tenant can will, sell or devise his or her piece as desired (no right of survivorship).

Termite Shield   A shield against termites built into new houses.

Title   Legal evidence of ownership of a property.

Title Company   A company which researches titles and usually also insures them against defects.

Title Insurance   Insurance obtained by the buyer of a house to insure against any undiscovered problems regarding the title to the property.

Title Search   An investigation into the history of ownership of a property to check for liens, unpaid claims, restrictions or problems, to prove that the seller can transfer free and clear ownership.

Veterans Administration (VA)   A government agency which guarantees mortgage loans with no down payment to qualified veterans.

Warranty   A protection plan for the repair or replacement of defective merchandise or workmanship.

THE NO NONSENSE HOUSE BUYING CHECK LIST

GENERAL

LOCATION

Schools _____

Churches or Synagogues _____

Shopping _____

Public Transportation _____

    Bus _____

    Train _____

    Trolley _____

Highways _____

    Accessibility _____

Entertainment _____

COMMUNITY SERVICES

Hospital _____

    Location _____

Fire Department _____

    Location _____

Police Department _____

    Location _____

NUISANCES

Noise _____

ZONING

Residential _____

Commercial _____

EXTERIOR OF HOUSE

SIZE OF HOUSE _____

STYLE OF HOUSE _____

SITUATION OF HOUSE ON LOT

Takes Advantage of Sun _____

Takes Advantage of View _____

DRAINAGE _____

SIZE OF LOT _____

PRIVACY _____

ROADWAY _____

Traffic _____

Ambulance Service _____

Trash Removal _____

Sewage _____

   Type of System _____

Snow Plowing _____

HAZARDS

Natural _____

Artificial _____

FUTURE APPRECIATION

Stability of Neighborhood _____

Individuality of Houses _____

WATER QUALITY

Cost _____

TAXES

State _____

City _____

Local _____

ASSESSMENTS _____

EASEMENTS _____

Private Street _____

Children's Safety _____

SIDEWALKS

Yes or No _____

AUTOMOBILES

Driveway _____

Private _____

Semi-Private _____

Public _____

On Street Parking _____

Off Street Parking _____

Carport _____

Garage _____

   one car or two cars _____

   automated garage doors _____

   separate entrance from garage to house _____

   "mud" room _____

RECREATIONAL FACILITIES

Public _____

Private _____

Location _____

Noise _____

Swimming Pool _____

    indoor/outdoor _____

    location _____

    noise _____

Sports

    tennis _____

    golf _____

    bicycle path _____

    racquetball _____

    squash _____

    basketball _____

    handball _____

    horseback riding _____

    jogging path _____

Children's Playground _____

Open or Enclosed _____

Safety of Access (stairs) _____

LAND

Amount _____

Privacy _____

Front Yard _____

Side Yard _____

    size _____

Rear Yard _____

    size _____

LAWNS AND PLANTINGS

Trees _____

Shrubbery _____

Flowers _____

MATERIAL

Wood _____

Stone _____

Brick _____

Vinyl siding _____

Aluminum siding _____

INTERIOR

GENERAL

Intercom System _____

Burglar Alarm System _____

ROOF

Material ―――――

Age ―――――

Condition ―――――

Leaks ―――――

DOWNSPOUTS AND ROOF GUTTERS

Number ―――――

Placement ―――――

SPLASH BLOCKS

Placement ―――――

Sufficient to keep water from house ―――――

PESTS

Termite Inspection Certificate ―――――

Termite Inspection Warranty ―――――

Termite Shield (new house) ―――――

TERRACES AND PORCHES

Location ―――――

Privacy ―――――

Front Yard ―――――

Number ―――――

Size ―――――

Fire Safety System ―――――

smoke detectors ―――――

fire alarms ―――――

General Safety ―――――

Automated Vacuum Cleaning system ―――――

Pre-wired for Telephone and Television Cable ―――――

Carpet ―――――

color ―――――

kind ―――――

texture ―――――

Hardwood Floors ―――――

PLASTER

Free of Cracks ―――――

Free of Stains ―――――

SOUNDPROOFING

PLUMBING

Works Well ―――――

Convenient ―――――

Quiet ―――――

Water Pressure ―――――

UTILITY COSTS

Gas ───────────

Electric ───────────

Other ───────────

INSULATION

(The R Factor is the measure of heating and cooling efficiency. The higher the R Factor, the more efficient.)

Minimum of R-19 in Walls ───────────

Minimum of R-30 in Ceiling ───────────

Heat Pumps ───────────

TEMPERATURE CONTROLS

Location ───────────

Convenience ───────────

HEATING AND AIR CONDITIONING

Type (best type depends on area) ───────────

electric ───────────

gas ───────────

oil ───────────

hot water ───────────

zoned or not ───────────

Sunlight ───────────

morning ───────────

afternoon ───────────

Privacy ───────────

from outside ───────────

from rest of house ───────────

DEN OR FAMILY ROOM

Size ───────────

Shape ───────────

Location ───────────

Fireplace ───────────

Windows ───────────

View ───────────

Sunlight ───────────

morning ───────────

afternoon ───────────

Privacy ───────────

DINING ROOM

Location ───────────

Size ───────────

Accessibility to Kitchen ───────────

WINDOWS

Wood Clad _____

Vinyl Clad _____

Insulated _____

   thermal breaks _____

Bay Windows _____

Storm Windows _____

Screen Windows _____

STAIRS

Number _____

Accessibility _____

Safety _____

CLOSETS

Number _____

Location _____

Built-ins closets and dressing areas _____

LIVING ROOM

Size _____

Shape _____

Fireplace _____

Windows _____

Windows _____

View _____

BEDROOMS

Number _____

location _____

size _____

closets _____

BATHROOMS

Number _____

Size _____

Materials _____

Shower _____

Bathtub _____

Vanity _____

Medicine Cabinet _____

Closet _____

Storage Space _____

MASTER BEDROOM

Size _____

Shape _____

Closets _____

Location ———————————
Privacy ———————————
Fireplace ———————————
Floor Covering ———————————
Wall Covering ———————————

MASTER BATHROOM

Size ———————————
Location ———————————
Materials Used ———————————
Bathtub ———————————
  whirlpool ———————————
  jacuzzi ———————————
Steam ———————————
Shower ———————————
Vanity ———————————
  double or single ———————————
  integrated sink bowls ———————————
Medicine Cabinet ———————————
Storage Space ———————————
Closet ———————————

KITCHEN

Size ———————————
  eat-in or not ———————————

self-cleaning ———————————
gas or electric ———————————
age ———————————
brand ———————————
warranty ———————————

Microwave ———————————
size ———————————
brand ———————————
warranty ———————————

Refrigerator-Freezer ———————————
size and capacity ———————————
brand ———————————
age ———————————
single or double door ———————————
frost-free ———————————
ice maker ———————————
warranty ———————————

Trash Compactor ———————————
brand ———————————
warranty ———————————

Dishwasher ———————————
brand ———————————
age ———————————
warranty ———————————

Floors

wood _____

linoleum _____

tile _____

Exhaust System _____

Work Space _____

Counter Tops _____

material _____

built-ins _____

warranty _____

Kitchen Cabinets

number _____

material _____

accessibility _____

warranty _____

Sink

material _____

size _____

single or double bowl _____

Built-in cutting boards _____

Appliances

Oven _____

single or double _____

LAUNDRY ROOM

Work Space _____

Clothes Washer and Dryer _____

brand _____

age _____

size _____

capacity _____

warranty _____

"MUD ROOM"

Location _____

STORAGE AREAS

Location _____

Attic _____

Garage _____

Closets _____

Basement _____

BASEMENT

Size _____

Finished or Not _____

Size _____

Bathroom _____

Dry? _____

Appendix A—Part I
APPLICATION FOR ALL CONVENTIONAL MORTGAGES

Federal National Mortgage Association

TRANSMITTAL SUMMARY

IDENTIFICATION

1 LOAN TYPE	2 APPROVAL REQUESTED	3 SUBMISSION TYPE
1 ☐ Conventional - SFPM 3 ☐ VA 2 ☐ Conventional - RRM	1 ☐ Property Only 3 ☐ Credit (Property Previously Approved) 2 ☐ Property and Credit	1 ☐ Prior Approval 3 ☐ Delegated Underwriting 2 ☐ Approval and Purchase

4 SUBMISSION NUMBER	5 PROPERTY ADDRESS			
	(Street Number)	(Street Name)	(Section)	(Unit)

6 CITY	7 STATE	8 ZIP CODE	9 PROJECT TYPE 1 ☐ PUD 3 ☐ DeMinimis PUD 2 ☐ Condo 4 ☐ Subdivision	10 PROJECT NO

11 BORROWER			12 CO-BORROWER		
(Last Name)	(Initial)		(Last Name)	(Initials)	

PROPOSED FINANCING

13 MORTGAGE TYPE	14 MORTGAGE AMOUNT	15 GUARANTY AMOUNT (VA Only)	16 UNGUARANTEED PORTION (VA Only)	17 LOAN/VALUE RATIO	18 INTEREST RATE	19 ORIGINAL TERM
1 ☐ First Mortgage 2 ☐	$	$	% of Value			(Mos)

PROPERTY

20 NUMBER OF UNITS	21 SALE PRICE	22 APPRAISED VALUE	23 REASONABLE VALUE (VA Only)	24 VALUE
	$	$	$	$

STABLE MONTHLY INCOME	PROPOSED MONTHLY PAYMENTS

	BORROWER	CO-BORROWER	TOTAL		
25 BASE INCOME $ _____	$ _____	$ _____		39 FIRST MORTGAGE P&I	$ _____
26 _____ (OTHER)	_____	_____		40 OTHER FINANCING	_____
27 _____ (OTHER)	_____	_____		41 HAZARD INSURANCE	_____
28 TOTAL INCOME $ _____	$ _____	$ _____		42 TAXES	_____

INCOME RATIOS - SINGLE FAMILY		43 MORTGAGE INSURANCE	_____
29 PAYMENT/INCOME RATIO _____ %		44 HOME OWNER ASSN. FEES	_____
30 OBLIGATIONS/INCOME RATIO _____ %		45 OTHER	_____

INCOME RATIOS - 2-4 FAMILY		46 TOTAL PAYMENT	$ _____
31 EFFECTIVE GROSS INCOME	$ _____	47 ALL OTHER MONTHLY PAYMENTS BEYOND 10 MONTHS (Including Applicable Alimony/Child Support)	
32 TOTAL OPERATING EXPENSES	(_____)		
33 OPERATING INCOME Subject Property (Line 31 Less Line 32)	$ _____	48 TOTAL ALL MONTHLY PAYMENTS	$ _____
34 25% OF LINE 28	$ _____	49 MONTHLY DEPOSITS TO IMPOUND ACCOUNTS FOR TAXES AND INSURANCE	1 ☐ Yes 2 ☐ No
35 PAYMENT/INCOME RATIO (Use Line 33 Plus Line 34 For Income)	_____ %		
36 33% OF LINE 28	$ _____	50 PROPERTY IS INTENDED TO BE THE PRIMARY RESIDENCE OF BORROWER OR CO-BORROWER	1 ☐ Yes 2 ☐ No
37 OBLIGATIONS/INCOME RATIO (Use Line 33 Plus Line 36 For Income)	_____ %		

38A	38B SATELLITE MORTGAGE ORGANIZATION

SELLER'S RECOMMENDATION

WE, THE UNDERSIGNED, HAVE UNDERWRITTEN AND RECOMMEND THAT YOU [☐ APPROVE / ☐ PURCHASE] THE SUBMISSION DESCRIBED ABOVE IN ACCORDANCE WITH THE TERMS OF OUR OUTSTANDING FNMA SELLING CONTRACT.

SELLER'S NAME _____

SELLER/SERVICER NUMBER _____

SELLER'S ADDRESS _____

UNDERWRITER SIGNATURE _____

UNDERWRITER NAME _____ NUMBER _____

TITLE _____ DATE _____

APPRAISER NAME _____ NUMBER _____

FOR RESPONSE TO THIS SUBMISSION REFER TO SELLER'S LOAN NUMBER	PERSON TO CALL (If Other Than Underwriter)	SELLER'S TELEPHONE NUMBER

DOCUMENTATION

IN ADDITION TO FNMA'S STANDARD DOCUMENTATION REQUIREMENTS, THE FOLLOWING EXHIBITS/COMMENTS ARE BEING FORWARDED IN SUPPORT OF THIS SUBMISSION:

EXHIBITS

A. _____

B. _____

C. _____

D. _____

UNDERWRITING CONSIDERATIONS

PROPERTY _____
_____
_____
_____
_____

MORTGAGOR APPLICANT(S) _____
_____
_____
_____
_____

DELEGATED UNDERWRITING ONLY: SPECIAL CONDITIONS/REQUIREMENTS SELLER IMPOSED FOR LOAN APPROVAL
_____
_____
_____
_____
_____

UPON REVIEW OF THIS SUBMISSION

FNMA REVIEWER
(SIGNATURE) _____ REVIEWER NUMBER _____ ACTION DATE __/__/__

A COMPLETED APPLICATION WAS RECEIVED BY FNMA ON _____
(DATE)

01☐ THE SUBMISSION HAS BEEN APPROVED

    SUBJECT TO THE FOLLOWING CONDITIONS:

    1☐ SELLER MUST INCLUDE WITH DELIVERY APPRAISER'S CERTIFICATION THAT PROPERTY WAS COMPLETED IN ACCORDANCE WITH PLANS AND SPECIFICATIONS AS IDENTIFIED ON APPRAISAL REPORT.

    2☐ SELLER MUST INCLUDE WITH DELIVERY ITS CERTIFICATION INDICATING REPAIRS TO THE PROPERTY AS STATED IN THE APPLICATION OR APPRAISAL REPORT HAVE BEEN SATISFACTORILY COMPLETED.

    3☐ SELLER MUST INCLUDE WITH DELIVERY EVIDENCE THAT SALE OF BORROWER'S PREVIOUS RESIDENCE HAS BEEN COMPLETED, RESULTING IN NET PROCEEDS OF $_____.

    4☐ OTHER: _____
_____
_____

02☐ THE SUBMISSION HAS BEEN RETURNED AT YOUR REQUEST

☐ THE SUBMISSION HAS BEEN DECLINED FOR THE REASON(S) STATED BELOW

CREDIT

03☐ NO CREDIT FILE

04☐ INSUFFICIENT CREDIT REFERENCES

05☐ INSUFFICIENT CREDIT FILE

06☐ UNABLE TO VERIFY CREDIT REFERENCES

07☐ GARNISHMENT, ATTACHMENT, FORECLOSURE, REPOSSESSION OR SUIT

08☐ INSUFFICIENT INCOME FOR TOTAL OBLIGATIONS

09☐ UNACCEPTABLE PAYMENT RECORD ON PREVIOUS MORTGAGE

10☐ LACK OF CASH RESERVES

11☐ DELINQUENT CREDIT OBLIGATIONS

12☐ BANKRUPTCY

☐ INFORMATION FROM A CONSUMER REPORTING AGENCY

ADDITIONAL COMMENTS: _____
_____
_____
_____

EMPLOYMENT STATUS

19☐ UNABLE TO VERIFY EMPLOYMENT

20☐ LENGTH OF EMPLOYMENT

21☐ INSUFFICIENT STABILITY OF INCOME

INCOME

24☐ INSUFFICIENT INCOME FOR MORTGAGE PAYMENTS

25☐ UNABLE TO VERIFY INCOME

RESIDENCY

28☐ SECONDARY RESIDENCE

PROPERTY

33☐ UNACCEPTABLE PROPERTY

34☐ INSUFFICIENT DATA-PROPERTY

35☐ UNACCEPTABLE APPRAISAL

36☐ UNACCEPTABLE LEASEHOLD ESTATE

OTHER

37☐ INSUFFICIENT FUNDS TO CLOSE THE LOAN

38☐ CREDIT APPLICATION INCOMPLETE

39☐ WE DO NOT GRANT CREDIT TO ANY APPLICANT ON THE TERMS AND CONDITIONS YOU REQUEST

FNMA Form 1008 Apr 80

Appendix A—Part II
APPLICATION TO QUALIFY FOR FHA MORTGAGE

U.S. DEPARTMENT OF HOUSING AND URBAN DEVELOPMENT HOUSING — FEDERAL HOUSING COMMISSIONER **MORTGAGE CREDIT ANALYSIS WORKSHEET**	CASE NUMBER

SECTION I — LOAN DATA

1. NAME OF BORROWER AND CO-BORROWER	2. AMOUNT OF MORTGAGE $	3. CASH DOWN PAYMENT ON PURCHASE PRICE $

SECTION II — BORROWER'S/CO-BORROWER'S PERSONAL AND FINANCIAL STATUS

4. BORROWER'S AGE	5. OCCUPATION OF BORROWER		6. NO. OF YRS. AT PRESENT ADDRESS	7. ASSETS AVAILABLE FOR CLOSING	8. CURRENT MONTHLY RENTAL OR OTHER HOUSING EXPENSE
9. IS CO-BORROWER EMPLOYED?	10. CO-BORROWER'S AGE	11. OCCUPATION OF CO-BORROWER	12. NO. OF YEARS AT PRESENT EMPLOYMENT	13. OTHER DEPENDENTS (a) Ages _____ (b) Number _____	

SECTION III — ESTIMATED MONTHLY SHELTER EXPENSES *(This Property)*	14. TERM OF LOAN *(Months)*	16. **SETTLEMENT REQUIREMENTS**	
		(a) Existing Debt *(Refinancing ONLY)*	$
15. (a) Principal and Interest	$	(b) Sale Price *(Realty ONLY)*	$
(b) FHA Mortgage Insurance Premium	$	(c) Repairs and Improvements	$
(c) Ground Rent *(Leasehold ONLY)*	$	(d) Closing Costs	$
(d) TOTAL DEBT SERVICE *(A + B + C)*	$	(e) TOTAL ACQUISITION COST *(A + B + C + D)*	$
(e) Hazard Insurance	$	(f) Mortgage Amount	$
(f) Taxes, Special Assessments	$	(g) Borrower(s)' Required Investment *(E minus F)*	$
(g) TOTAL MTG. PAYMENT *(D + E + F)*	$	(h) Prepayable Expenses	$
(h) Maintenance and Common Expense	$	(i) Non-Realty and Other Items	$
(i) Heat and Utilities	$	(j) TOTAL REQUIREMENTS *(G + H + I)*	$
(j) TOTAL HSG. EXPENSE *(G + H + I)*	$	(k) Amount paid ☐ cash ☐ other *(explain)*	$
(k) Other Recurring Charges *(explain)*	$	(l) Amt. to be paid ☐ cash ☐ other *(explain)*	$
(l) TOTAL FIXED PAYMENT *(j + K)*	$	(m) TOTAL ASSETS AVAILABLE FOR CLOSING	$

SECTION IV — MONTHLY EFFECTIVE INCOME		SECTION V — DEBTS AND OBLIGATIONS			
		ITEM	✓	Monthly Payment	Unpaid Balance
17. Borrower's Base Pay	$	25. State and Local Income Taxes		$	$
18. Other Earnings *(explain)*	$	26. Social Security/Retirement			
19. Co-Borrower's Base Pay	$	27.			
20. Other Earnings *(explain)*	$	28.			
21. Income, Real Estate	$	29.			
22. TOTAL MONTHLY EFFECTIVE INCOME	$	30.			
23. Less Federal Tax	$	31.			
24. NET EFFECTIVE INCOME	$				

SECTION VI — BORROWER RATING		32.			
34. Borrower Rating		33.	TOTAL	$	$
35. Credit Characteristics		39. FINAL	40. Loan to Value Ratio ____ %	43. ☐ Ratio of Net Effective Income to:	
36. Adequacy of Eff. Income		☐ Approve Application			
37. Stability of Eff. Income		☐ Reject Application	41. Total Payment to Rental Value ____ %	Total Housing Expense ____ %	
38. Adequacy of Available Assets			42. Debt Service to Rental Income ____ %	Total Fixed Payment ____ %	
44. REMARKS *(Use reverse, if necessary)*	First Time Home Buyer? ☐ Yes ☐ No				

(SECTION VII — RATIOS)

45. SIGNATURE OF EXAMINER	46. DATE

RETAIN ORIGINAL IN CASE BINDER, FORWARD COPY TO MANAGEMENT
INFORMATION SYSTEMS DIVISION WITH HUD-92900-8

HUD-92900-WS (5-81)

APPENDIX B
GOOD FAITH ESTIMATE OF SETTLEMENT COSTS

Colonial Name _____

Branch Office Address _____

Telephone Number _____

GOOD FAITH ESTIMATE OF SETTLEMENT COSTS

APPLICANT(S) _____ DATE _____

PROPERTY ADDRESS _____

SALES PRICE _____ LOAN AMOUNT _____

NOTICE - THIS FORM DOES NOT COVER ALL ITEMS YOU WILL BE REQUIRED TO PAY IN CASH AT
SETTLEMENT, FOR EXAMPLE, DEPOSIT IN ESCROW FOR REAL ESTATE TAXES AND INSURANCE.
YOU MAY WISH TO INQUIRE AS TO THE AMOUNT OF OTHER SUCH ITEMS. YOU MAY BE REQUIRED
TO PAY OTHER ADDITIONAL AMOUNTS AT SETTLEMENT

THIS GOOD FAITH ESTIMATE OF SETTLEMENT COSTS IS MADE PURSUANT TO THE REQUIREMENTS
OF THE REAL ESTATE SETTLEMENT PROCEDURES ACT. THESE FIGURES ARE ONLY ESTIMATES
AND THE ACTUAL CHARGES DUE AT SETTLEMENT MAY BE DIFFERENT.

L. SETTLEMENT CHARGES		AMOUNT
800. ITEMS PAYABLE IN CONNECTION WITH THE LOAN		
801. Loan Origination Fee	%	$
802. Loan Discount	%	
803. Appraisal Fee		
804. Credit Report Fee		
805. Lender's Inspection Fee		
806. Mortgage Insurance Application Fee		
807. Assumption Fee		
808. Application Fee		
809. VA Funding Fee		
810. HUD Mortgage Insurance Premium		
811.		
900. ITEMS REQUIRED BY LENDER TO BE PAID IN ADVANCE		
901. Interest from to @ /day		
902. Mortgage Insurance Premium for months to		
1100. TITLE CHARGES		
1101. Settlement or closing fee		
1102. Abstract or Title search		
1103. Title Examination		
1104. Title Insurance Binder		
1105. Document Preparation		
1106. Notary Fees		
1107. Attorney's fees (including above items numbers;)		
1108. Title Insurance (including above items numbers;)		
1109. Lender's Coverage		
1110. Owner's Coverage		
1111. Endorsement(s):		
1112.		
1200. GOVERNMENT RECORDING AND TRANSFER CHARGES		
1201. Recording Fees: Deed $ Mortgage $ Release $		
1202. City/County Tax/Stamps Deed $ Mortgage $		
1203. State Tax/Stamps Deed $ Mortgage $		
1204.		
1300. ADDITIONAL SETTLEMENT CHARGES		
1301. Survey		
1302. Pest Inspection		
1303. Amortization Schedule		
1304.		
1305.		
TOTAL ESTIMATED SETTLEMENT CHARGES		$

I HEREBY ACKNOWLEDGE THAT I HAVE RECEIVED A COPY OF THIS GOOD FAITH ESTIMATE OF
SETTLEMENT COSTS AND A COPY OF THE HUD GUIDE FOR HOME BUYERS "SETTLEMENT COSTS AND
YOU".

_____ _____ _____ _____
APPLICANT'S SIGNATURE   DATE   APPLICANT'S SIGNATURE   DATE

IF MAILED, BY: _____
                                                          _____
                                                           DATE

(G15A)

APPENDIX C

A.

DISCLOSURE/SETTLEMENT STATEMENT
U.S. DEPARTMENT OF HOUSING AND URBAN DEVELOPMENT · APRIL '75

B. TYPE OF LOAN

1. ☐ FHA 2. ☐ FMHA 3. ☐ CONV. UNINS.
4. ☐ VA 5. ☐ CONV. INS.

6. FILE NUMBER   7. LOAN NUMBER

If the Truth-in-Lending Act applies to this transaction, a Truth-in-Lending statement is attached as page 3 of this form.

8. MORTG. INS. CASE NO.

C. NOTE: This form is furnished to you prior to settlement to give you information about your settlement costs, and again after settlement to show the actual costs you have paid. The present copy of the form is:

STATEMENT OF ACTUAL COSTS. Amounts paid to and by the settlement agent are shown. Items marked *"(p.o.c.)"* were paid outside the closing; they are shown here for informational purposes and are not included in totals.

D. NAME OF BORROWER   **E. SELLER**   **F. LENDER**

G. PROPERTY LOCATION   **H. SETTLEMENT AGENT**   **I. DATES**

LOAN COMMITMENT | ADVANCE DISCLOSURE

PLACE OF SETTLEMENT | SETTLEMENT | DATE OF PRORATIONS IF DIFFERENT FROM SETTLEMENT

J. SUMMARY OF BORROWER'S TRANSACTION	K. SUMMARY OF SELLER'S TRANSACTION
100. GROSS AMOUNT DUE FROM BORROWER:	**400. GROSS AMOUNT DUE TO SELLER:**
101. Contract sales price	401. Contract sales price
102. Personal property	402. Personal property
103. Settlement charges to borrower (from line 1400, Section L)	403.
104.	404.
105.	**Adjustments for items paid by seller in advance:**
Adjustments for items paid by seller in advance:	405. City/town taxes to
106. City/town taxes to	406.
107.	407.
108.	408. Water to
109. Water to	409. Sewer to
110. Sewer to	410. to
111. to	411. to
112. to	**420. GROSS AMOUNT DUE TO SELLER**
120. GROSS AMOUNT DUE FROM BORROWER:	**500. REDUCTIONS IN AMOUNT DUE TO SELLER:**
	501. Deposit or earnest money received
200. AMOUNTS PAID BY OR IN BEHALF OF BORROWER:	502. Payoff of first mortgage loan
201. Deposit or earnest money	
202. Principal amount of new loan(s)	503. Payoff of second mortgage loan
203. Existing loan(s) taken subject to	
204.	504. Settlement charges to seller (from line 1400, Section L)
205.	
Credits to borrower for items unpaid by seller:	505. Existing loan(s) taken subject to
	506.
206. City/town taxes to	507.
207.	508
208.	509
209. Water to	
210. Sewer to	
211. to	**Credits to buyer for items unpaid by seller:**
212. to	510. City/town taxes to
220. TOTAL AMOUNTS PAID BY OR IN BEHALF OF BORROWER	511. to
	512. to
300. CASH AT SETTLEMENT REQUIRED FROM OR PAYABLE TO BORROWER:	513. Water to
	514. Sewer to ,
301. Gross amount due from borrower (from line 120)	515. to
	520. TOTAL REDUCTIONS IN AMOUNT DUE TO SELLER:
302. Less amounts paid by or in behalf of borrower (from line 220)	**600. CASH TO SELLER FROM SETTLEMENT:**
	601. Gross amount due to seller (from line 420)
303. CASH (☐ REQUIRED FROM) OR	602. Less total reductions in amount due to seller (from line 520)
(☐ PAYABLE TO) BORROWER:	**603. CASH TO SELLER FROM SETTLEMENT**

L. SETTLEMENT CHARGES	PAID FROM BORROWER'S FUNDS	PAID FROM SELLER'S FUNDS
700. SALES BROKER'S COMMISSION based on price $ @ %		
701. Total commission paid by seller		
Division of commission as follows:		
702. $ to		
703. $ to		
704.		
800. ITEMS PAYABLE IN CONNECTION WITH LOAN		
801. Loan Origination fee %		
802. Loan Discount %		
803. Appraisal Fee to		
804. Credit Report to		
805. Lender's inspection fee		
806. Mortgage insurance application fee to		
807. Assumption fee		
808.		
809.		
810.		
811.		
900. ITEMS REQUIRED BY LENDER TO BE PAID IN ADVANCE.		
901. Interest from to @ $ /day		
902. Mortgage insurance premium for mo. to		
903. Hazard insurance premium for yrs. to		
904.		
905.		
1000. RESERVES DEPOSITED WITH LENDER FOR:		
1001. Hazard insurance mo. @ $ /mo.		
1002. Mortgage insurance mo. @ $ /mo.		
1003. City property taxes mo. @ $ /mo.		
1004. County property taxes mo. @ $ /mo.		
1005. Annual assessments mo. @ $ /mo.		
1006. mo. @ $ /mo.		
1007.		
1008.		
1100. TITLE CHARGES:		
1101. Settlement or closing fee to		
1102. Abstract or title search to		
1103. Title examination to		
1104. Title insurance binder to		
1105. Document preparation to		
1106. Notary fees to		
1107. Attorney's Fees to		
(includes above items No.:		
1108. Title insurance to		
(includes above items No.:		
1109. Lender's coverage $		
1110. Owner's coverage $		
1111.		
1112.		
1113.		
1200. GOVERNMENT RECORDING AND TRANSFER CHARGES		
1201. Recording fees: Deed $; Mortgage $ Release $		
1202.		
1203. State tax/stamps: Deed $ to:		
1204.		
1300. ADDITIONAL SETTLEMENT CHARGES		
1301. Survey to		
1302. Pest inspection to		
1303.		
1304.		
1305.		
1400. TOTAL SETTLEMENT CHARGES (entered on lines 103 and 503, Sections J and K)		

NOTE: Under certain circumstances the borrower and seller may be permitted to waive the 12-day period which must normally occur between advance disclosure and settlement. In the event such a waiver is made, copies of the statements of waiver, executed as provided in the regulations of the Department of Housing and Urban Development, shall be attached to and made a part of this form when the form is used as a settlement statement.

Seller		Purchaser
Seller		Purchaser
Address	Address	

ABOUT THE AUTHORS

PHYLLIS C. KAUFMAN, the originator of the *No Nonsense Guides*, is a Philadelphia attorney and theatrical producer. A graduate of Brandeis University, she was an editor of the law review at Temple University School of Law. She is listed in *Who's Who in American Law*, *Who's Who of American Women*, and *Foremost Women of the Twentieth Century*.

ARNOLD CORRIGAN, noted financial expert, is the author of *How Your IRA Can Make You a Millionaire* and is a frequent guest on financial talk shows. A senior officer of a large New York investment advisory firm, he holds Bachelor's and Master's degrees in economics from Harvard and has written for *Barron's* and other financial publications.